ISBN 978-1-334-10813-6
PIBN 10581676

English
Français
Deutsche
Italiano
Español
Português

www.forgottenbooks.com

Mythology Photography **Fiction**
Fishing Christianity **Art** Cooking
Essays Buddhism Freemasonry
Medicine **Biology** Music **Ancient**
Egypt Evolution Carpentry Physics
Dance Geology **Mathematics** Fitness
Shakespeare **Folklore** Yoga Marketing
Confidence Immortality Biographies
Poetry **Psychology** Witchcraft
Electronics Chemistry History **Law**
Accounting **Philosophy** Anthropology
Alchemy Drama Quantum Mechanics
Atheism Sexual Health **Ancient History**
Entrepreneurship Languages Sport
Paleontology Needlework Islam
Metaphysics Investment Archaeology
Parenting Statistics Criminology
Motivational

Era

Organ of the Priesthood Quorums, the Young Men's Mutual Improvement
Associations, and the Schools of the Church of Jesus Christ of Latter-day Saints
Published monthly by the General Board Y. M. M. I. A., Salt Lake City, Utah

Characteristic Sayings of President Lorenzo Snow

The reward for righteousness is exaltation.

Godliness cannot be conferred, but must be acquired.

We approach godliness as fast as we approach perfection.

Before I die, I hope to see the Church cleared of debt and in a commanding position financially.

If we are faithful, we shall at some time do our own work, but now we are doing the work of our Father.

The Lord has shown me most clearly and completely that Joseph Smith was a prophet of God.

Greater work was never done by man since the days of Adam than is being done here in the temple.

We have all the possibilities of God himself, and we should so act that every faculty shall be developed to the utmost.

A mother who has brought up a family of faithful children ought to be saved, if she never does another good thing.

The glorious opportunity of becoming truly great belongs to every faithful elder in Israel; it is his by right divine.

Before the lion and the lamb shall lie down together in peace man must desist from hunting, killing and eating the flesh of animals.

I would like to live to see the time when the old bitterness between "Mormons" and non-"Mormons" shall have disappeared.

Man may become like his Father, doing the works which his Father did before him, and he cannot be deprived of the opportunity of reaching this exalted state.

The destiny of man is to be like his Father—a god in eternity. This should be a bright, illuminating star before him all the time—in his heart, in his soul, and all through him.

> As man now is, God once was:
> As God now is, man may be.
>
> A son of God, like God to be,
> Would not be robbing Deity.

LORENZO SNOW

Fifth President of the Church of Jesus Christ of Latter-day Saints.

In referring to the death, a short time before, of Elder King Follett, the Prophet preached a general funeral sermon. This was one of his last sermons, as the martyrdom occurred less than three months later. This sermon was first published, in part, about six weeks after the martyrdom, in the August 15, 1844, issue of the *Times and Seasons,* and seventeen years afterward, in 1861, it appeared in Vol. 23 of the *Millennial Star.* It was also printed in the January number of the *Improvement Era,* in 1909, with explanatory footnotes by Elder B. H. Roberts.

The King Follett sermon, as it is called, was reported by Willard Richards, Wilford Woodruff, Thomas Bullock and William Clayton in longhand. After its first publication, in 1844, it was revised and corrected before its publication in 1861. While absolutely no change is made in this thought of the destiny of man, the later wording is clearer and better and is a result of careful comparison and consideration by those who reported and heard the discourse. (For further explanation, see *History of the Church,* Vol. 4, page 556; Vol. 6, pp. 248-54.)

There are two references in this sermon to the idea of the possible progress and development of man, which I quote both from the *Times and Seasons* and from the *Millennial Star,* the words in italics having been added in the later publication:

Times and Seasons, Aug. 15, 1844.

First, God himself, who sits enthroned in yonder heavens, is a man like unto one of yourselves, that is the great secret. If the vail was rent today, and the great God, who holds this world in its orbit, and upholds all things by his power; if you were to see him today, you would see him in all the person, image and very form as a man; for Adam was created in the very fashion and image of God; Adam received instruction, walked, talked and conversed with him, as one man talks and communes with another.

These are incomprehensible ideas to some, but they are the simple and first principles of the gospel, to know for a certainty the character of God, that we may converse with him as one man with another, and that God himself, the Father of us all, dwelt on an earth the same as Jesus Christ himself did, and I will show it from the Bible.

Millennial Star, 1861

God himself was once as we are now. And is an exalted Man, and sits enthroned in yonder heavens! That is the great secret. If the vail were rent today, and the great God who holds this world in its orbit, and who upholds all worlds and all things by his power, was to make himself visible,—I say, if you were to see him today, you would see him like a man in form—like yourselves in all the person, image, and very form as a man; for Adam was created in the very fashion, image and likeness of God, and received instruction from, and walked, talked and conversed with him, as one man talks and communes with another.

These are incomprehensible ideas to some, but they are simple. It is the first principle of the gospel to know for a certainty the character of God, and to know that we may converse with him as one man converses with another, *and that he was once a man like us;* yea, that God himself, the Father of us all, dwelt on an earth, the same as Jesus Christ himself did; and I will show it from the Bible.

In President Snow's own copy of the *Times and Seasons,* which I now have, he drew more particular attention, with his own indelible pencil, to this part of the Prophet's King Follett sermon than to any other reference in all the six volumes. This great hope in man's destiny, through strict obedience to the gospel, was in his mind so constantly that he frequently referred to it in the home circle, in his public discourses, both when addressing aged parents and when talkng to little children, and many of his intimate friends know that it was a favorite theme in private and confidential conversations.

Few comparisons were more frequently repeated by President Snow in his public speaking than the following:

As an illustration, here is an infant upon its mother's breast. It is without power or knowledge to feed and clothe itself. It is so helpless that it has to be fed by its mother. But see its possibilities! This infant has a father and a mother, though it knows scarcely anything about them. Who is its father? Who is its mother? Why, its father is an emperor, its mother is an empress, and they sit upon a throne, governing an empire. This little infant will some day, in all probability, sit upon his father's throne, and govern and control the empire, just as King Edward of England now sits upon the throne of his mother. We should have this in mind; for we are the sons of God, as much so and more, if possible, than we are the sons of our earthly fathers.

You sisters, I suppose, have read that poem which my sister, Eliza R. Snow Smith, composed, years ago, and which is sung quite frequently now in our meetings. It tells us that we not only have a Father in "that high and glorious place," but that we have a Mother, too; and you sisters will become as great as your Mother, if you are faithful.

Only a short time before his death, President Snow visited the Brigham Young University, at Provo. President Brimhall escorted the party through one of the buildings; he wanted to reach the assembly room as soon as possible, as the students had already gathered. They were going through one of the kindergarten rooms; President Brimhall had reached the door and was about to open it and go on when President Snow said: "Wait a moment, President Brimhall, I want to see these children at work; what are they doing?" Brother Brimhall replied that they were making clay spheres. "That is very interesting," the President said. "I want to watch them." He quietly watched the children for several minutes and then lifted a little girl, perhaps six years of age, and stood her on a table. He then took the clay sphere from her hand, and, turning to Brother Brimhall, said:

President Brimhall, these children are now at play, making mud worlds, the time will come when some of these boys, through their faithfulness to

I have a testimony of the gospel of Jesus Christ, which has given me a better understanding of things pertaining to life. It has caused me to have greater love and appreciation for my beloved brothers and sisters and friends. Man is my brother, woman is my sister, and I owe them as much respect as I would owe my sisters and brothers of my own kin. Why? Because they are my brothers and sisters in the Spirit of the Almighty. For the glorious opportunity that I have had to gain a beautiful testimony I am thankful. On account of my affliction, I have been taken through many trials and tribulations. I have been made to humble myself before God, and I have let him know all about my sorrows and my desires. He has comforted my aching heart with his Holy Spirit.

I was the first one in my father's family to go down into the waters of baptism; others have followed me. I have heard the testimony of the servants of the Lord, and of some of the old pioneers. O! I honor those dear old pioneers who laid down their lives for the gospel, and for their children and their children's children, that they might enjoy the gospel and gain salvation in the kingdom of our heavenly Father. I honor them because they builded homes, canals, roads and bridges, in these beautiful valleys of these everlasting hills.

I honor the Prophet Joseph Smith and his brother Hyrum. I love to sustain and know the leaders of our Church of today, because they are inspired men of the Lord, to lead and direct the Church.

I love Old Glory because she is the banner of the greatest Nation in all the world, and I love and honor the boys who have been fighting for Liberty and Freedom.

I pray that we may all live so that we can be worthy Latter-day Saints, and good, loyal American citizens.

Digging the Dinosaur in Utah

By J. Cecil Alter, Meteorologist, U. S. Department of Agriculture, Weather Bureau

Looking back through the ages, some fifteen million years, the geologist sees the plateau lands of Utah at sea-level, her lakes and hills smiling in summery air; while the paleontologist sees hereabouts an order of gigantic beasts which he has named *Dinosauria*, striding leisurely and awkwardly over the well-wooded lands, and feeding peacefully along the shore waters of the lakes.

Some members of this genealogical group, such as the armored *Stegosaurus*, weighed only a possible six or eight tons, the lizard-like body of which arched upward fifteen feet from the ground and was some twenty-five feet in total length. This individual had a comparatively short neck and tail, though some of his relatives having similarly unique bodies, were about one-third head and neck, one-third body, and one-third a heavy, tapering tail. Other members of this group, like the *Diplodocus* and the *Brontosaurus*, were mastodonian monarchs nearly a hundred feet in length, weighing perhaps twenty or twenty-five tons, or five or six times as much as a large elephant.

But while we contemplate the wonderful spectacle in imagination of a herd of these monsters shambling out of the shady forests for a sublime splash in the cooling lake, we feel and hear the thunderous reverberations of their running, which blends, historically at least, with the rumblings of the earth's interior, when the present lands of Utah were lifted to their exalted elevation, and perhaps brought on a change of climate through changes in the earth's orientation, or otherwise, which in turn caused the destruction of the lakes, and the so-called thunder lizards. The *Dinosaurs'* bodies, with the flesh on, undoubtedly floated with the water currents, until they became grounded on the shallow places or near the water's edge, there to be buried in sand and mud which later became the sandstone in which they are found entombed.

The land upon which those lizards lived, when found in strata by present-day geologists, is referred to Mesozoic times, or the age of reptiles, while the soil and sands about the remains of the giant animals, has been called Comanchean or Lower Cretaceous sandstone, for stone it has become by reason of great age and pressure due to subsequent earth layers. Most of these strata are hundreds, if not thousands of feet beneath. Utah's present surface, but where subsequent uplifts have occurred there is exposed a succession of layers of the earth's crust; and where the deep Jurassic, or the Cretaceous above it, has been brought up, exposing areas where the *Dinosaurs* congregated or were forced to assemble before or after their destruction, the broad leaves of the book of the past open somewhat reluctantly,

Left—Mineralized fibula of Stegosaurus. Probably the owner of the bone showing in the face of the rock beneath the man's hands in the view, was about 35 feet long, 15 feet high, being one-third head and neck, one-third body, and one-third tail, the latter being large and tapering, like a lizard's tail. This bone has probably been exposed in the weather for many centuries.

Right—View looking east along the sandstone ledge, 10 to 15 feet wide, which carries the fossils. Professor Douglas leans against the north limit of the quarry; many broken bones lie about his feet; not broken in his work, which has been extremely careful, but broken when they lodged in the quarry ages ago—he is now removing the plaster-cast of sand stone which Nature tried to cover them with. When he gets a good bone, he in turn puts it in another plaster-burlap cast for shipping, as shown just beyond him in the view. The workman is chiseling away the sandstone very carefully from a bone he has found.

and reveal a part of the wonderful story of prehistoric life on earth.

The leaves of the book, the earth's strata, though considerably frayed and weather-worn, are nevertheless quite widely open, and their contents most plainly visible, near Split Mountain Canyon, above the majestic Lonetree Bend in the Green River, four or five miles due north of Jensen, Uintah county,

In the Dinosaur District

(For descriptions, see opposite page.)

Top—At work at Carnegie Museum Dinosaur Quarry. Shows pelvis, femur and other bones of skeleton exposed. A man is at work behind the femur, which is nearly in place.

Middle—Professor Earl Douglas, paleontologist, Carnegie Museum, for 10 years in charge of excavations at The Dinosaur National Monument, near Jensen, Utah. He is now a legal resident of Utah, on a homestead taken up near his pets, the entombed prehistoric animals. He is seated on a face of sandstone carrying several more or less detached dinosaur bones, showing on both sides of him. His genial smile, born of his great optimism and enthusiasm which have made the work possible, has won many friends in his new home; no one finds in him anything distant or unlikable.

Bottom—Dinosaur National Monument, and Split Mountain Canyon, in distance, and Lonetree Bend, Green River, Utah, view northeast, from point four miles due north from Jensen, Uintah county (lower northeastern part).

Utah. And here, for ten eventful years, the thought and interest of the leading paleontologists of the world have centered, while Professor Earl Douglas and a corps of skilled assistants have lifted from their stony bed many heavy mineralized skeletons, remains of life in that wonderful long ago.

It was eleven years ago that the Carnegie Museum sent Professor Douglas to the Uintah Basin to collect fossil mammals from the Uintah Tertiary deposits. The first camp was established in a stone cabin at Well No. 2, near the present shearing plant at Bonanza station, on the Uintah railway. In August of that year (1908) Dr. William J. Holland, of the Carnegie Institute and Museum, visited the camp, and with Dr. Douglas drove to a place on the Green River, northeast of Jensen, where Mr. B. Burton, a prospector, had previously shown Dr. Douglas some *Dinosaur* bones.

Dr. Holland thought it would not pay to do much excavating here, but wished to secure two or three of the large scattering limb-bones. However, the expedition was so successful in securing fossil mammals that there was no time to excavate for *Dinosaur* bones. In 1909 Dr. Douglas was sent again to the Uintah Basin to make further explorations for fossil mammals and for *Dinosaurs* from the so-called Jurassic beds. (Often called Jurassic, the geological enigma is not yet settled; Comanchean or Lower Cretaceous it more probably is, according to Dr. Douglas.) The formation is the one which was called Como by Marsh.

After searching this Como formation for about two weeks, and doing some excavating without any satisfactory results, on August 19, 1909, Dr. Douglas came upon seven large tail vertebrae weathered out in relief on a sandstone cliff. These bones now form a part of a skeleton mounted on its feet in the Carnegie Museum, in Pittsburg, a *Brontosaurus* which in its living days was almost the equal in size of the *Gigantosaurus*, the African monster which was probably the king of prehistoric animal life on earth. This specimen, mounted, is about eighty feet in length; however, a section of missing tail vertebrae was interpolated, in this one, but later, when a complete specimen, in respect to the tail, was found, it was discovered that the interpolated tail was more than ten feet too short, which will necessitate the enlargement of the mounting and the exhibit rooms, to restore it to its true size.

Head of femur of a Brontosaurus, probably one of the largest specimens of the world's largest prehistoric animals. This detached part of bone was found in the quarry near Jensen, Utah, and is on exhibit at the Commercial Club at Vernal. Being mineralized, it is many times heavier than bone, weighing as much as the heavier rock.

It required twenty-six four-horse teams to transport the first shipment of disarticulated skeletons sixty miles to the railroad station at Dragon. It required two years to disinter the fossilized bones and prepare them for shipment, and four or more years to remove the plaster-of-Paris matrices used for shipping protection, and the clinging scraps of sandstone, and mount the first large skeleton at the Carnegie Museum.

The work done in taking up this skeleton uncovered portions of several other skeletons. The work was continued, and new skeletons, and portions of skeletons, a greater part of which are new to science, have been coming to light ever since. All skeletons are more or less incomplete, though it has often been easy to supply many missing parts by interpolation or by substitution from the great mass of disconnected parts, representing scores, if not hundreds, of animals of all sizes. Dr. Douglas has seldom left the *Dinosaur* quarry in these eleven years, preferring to remain in closest touch with the workings to assure the greatest possible success in assembling the scattered remains. In fact, he has established his legal residence and permanent home on a homestead near the quarry.

There have been times when for months there were no large nor perfect skeletons, intact, coming to light, yet the work has been continued with great patience and labor. As a result of this perseverance, Dr. Douglas writes (March 12, 1919): "We are still working here, getting out the most complete skeleton we have ever taken up. This specimen, complete, will be secured during this summer."

A visit to the quarry is not without its disappointments, as one is apt to expect too much of a spectacular nature. The many colored rocks, clays and standstones, for some square miles to the north, representing strata many thousands of years

Freight outfit which hauled Dinosaur bones from quarry in northeastern Utah, to railroad, and returned with supplies.

older than the Jurassic, and the flint ledge to the south, all decorated with the artistic cedar clumps, and skirted by the sinuous, stream, makes it a beautiful region; and its dry climate makes it attractive most of the year. But one requires the eye of faith, and the spiritual intuition of the patient paleontologist in order to visualize the major facts at hand from the views presented about the quarry itself.

The exposed seam, or layer, carrying the fossils, is about a half mile in length, running about east-west approximately a mile north of the river, the trend being towards Split Mountain Canyon. However, while prehistorical animal signs have been

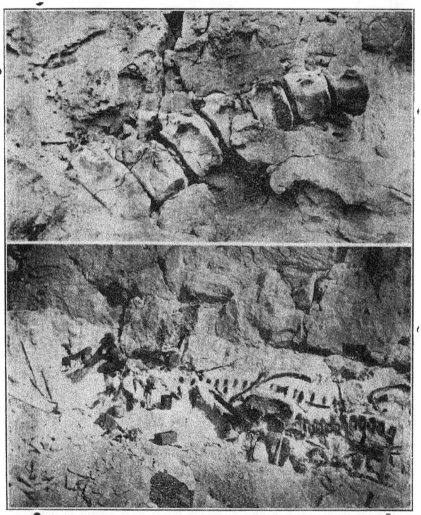

Showing Skeleton Bones in the Rock Layer, at Jensen, Utah

found, here and there, in the entire seam, there are only two important sections or ridges in the line, not carried away by cross erosion in lateral gulleys, where there are important deposits of the fossils. Only one of these places has been explored more than superficially, this crest being only a few hundred feet

"Henry," he said as the clerk appeared in the doorway, "I shall be detained here some time with Mr. Pygus, so you needn't wait. Good night. Now Squire," he went on, turning to Pygus, as the door of the outer office slammed and the sound of footsteps died away down the corridor.

"I've come to talk business," Pygus repeated. He paused and chewed furiously for a time in meditative silence. "Oil business," he at length said pointedly.

Sanderson's face clouded.

"And what about the oil business, Squire?" he asked, a trifle impatiently.

"What are you willin' to pay for stock in the Pennsylvania Oil Company just now?" Pygus asked.

Sanderson's smile was one of patient condescension.

"The fact is, Squire, the Pennsylvania didn't turn out just as we expected," he explained. "All around us the wells are making all kinds of money, but somehow or other our holdings are as dry as sawdust."

Squire Pygus fixed his eyes doubtfully on the brass cuspidor at his feet.

"Look ahere, Jim," he said, "you must be drove pretty hard when you take to skinnin' your own townfolks."

The other's face hardened. "Those are pretty bald words you're using, Judge," he said, drawing himself up in his chair and fixing his eyes on the man opposite.

"I know it, Jim," Pygus declared regretfully, "but I weighed 'em before I said 'em, an', take it by an' large, they represent about the sum total of it. Us folks at the Lower Corners ain't so all-fired green that we're bitin' at every get-rich-quick scheme that comes out in the papers, but when we got them prospectuses an' circulars you sent us it was different. You was born an' raised there—a Sanderson of the Lower Corners, an' none of us never knew of a Sanderson goin' back on his word. Naturally, we thought that, comin' from you, we was gettin' it straight."

In the Squire's tone there was more of sorrow than anger. He lifted his eyes and looked searchingly at Sanderson, who twisted uneasily in his chair.

"See here," the latter burst out hotly—and he was plainly on the defensive now—"I'm telling you the truth, Squire, when I say I thought we'd hit the bull's eye with that oil-land. I wanted to let you people in on the ground floor. Don't I know the Lower Corners, and don't I know how hard the money comes there? I couldn't make that land pump oil if there wasn't any there."

He paused. The Squire's eyes were still on him, their steadfast disapproval causing him extreme discomfort.

"But I'll tell you what I'll do for you, Squire, if you'll say nothing about it," he went on hurriedly. "If you'll tell me just what you put into it, for old sake's sake, I'll make you out a check for the amount."

, A flash of fire leaped to the Squire's eyes. He brought down one huge fist with a bang on the corner of the desk.

"You don't think that's what I come down here for, do ye?" he roared. "I should o' thought you'd known me better than that, Jim Sanderson. I ain't sayin' nothin' how I got bit. What I put in I could afford to lose an' count it money gone for experience. But the part that gets me is what the others done—old Miss Watson drawin' her money out of the savin's bank, an' Uncle Benjamin Hopkins mortgagin' his place, to git money to put into your scheme, an' dozens of others just like 'em—all of 'em doin' it because they know'd you were a Sanderson."

"Good Lord," cried Sanderson. "You don't expect me to make good to all those people, who took their chances just as I did, do you?"

"I ain't askin' you to," said Pygus flatly.

"Then what is it you want me to do?"

"I came down here today with a fixed purpose in my mind," said Pygus, lapsing once more into a drawl. He hooked the brass cuspidor toward him with his foot and spat into it reflectively.

"A good many years ago, Jim, when you an' I was boys, I traded you an A-1 first class fiddle for a watch that you said was all right. Now, if you remember, that watch was sort of misrepresented. The mainspring was broke, an' both of the hands were loose."

He paused. Sanderson gravely nodded his head.

"I want you to think a minute, Jim," Pygus went on, "an' see 'f you can't remember what I done to you when I found out what shape that watch was in."

Sanderson chuckled shamefacedly. "As near as I can remember, Squire," said he, "you gave me the all-firedest drubbing I ever had in my life."

"Right you are, sonny," Pygus exclaimed. He arose, and his gaunt old frame towered beside the desk. "Now, doin' it again, I'm perfectly aware, won't bring back the money that you've skinned out of the folks at the Lower Corners, but all the same I'm goin' to do it, jest to let you know that you can't cheat folks now any more than you could then an' git off free."

He pulled off his coat and vest and tossed them into a corner.

"Jim Sanderson," he thundered, "stand up. Stand up, I tell yer, an' don't sit there with your mouth open like that, for by the livin' fishes, I'm goin' to do jest as I say."

Slowly a sickly, incredulous grin spread over Sanderson's face. He pushed back his chair, but made no motion to rise,

ly, and when Lee and Lillywhite took their guns and went out into the yard, in front of the house, they were fired upon by Indians. Lillywhite was shot through the right breast, and staggering back into the house fell helpless. Lee, after discharging his gun at the Indians, retreated to the house, where he barricaded the doors and windows, and made such preparations as were possible for defense. The Indians piled brush and poles against the house and set fire to it, by which the roof was ignited, and it looked for a short time as if the building would be destroyed, but there was a large quantity of milk in the room, and the flames were finally brought under control by throwing milk upon them. An Indian, using the handle of a pitchfork,

Cedar Knoll

succeeded in prying open the door, when Lee shot him. Another exposed himself at a window and was likewise shot.

While the fight was in progress, a boy eight years old, and his sister, younger, were put out of the house through a window where bushes grew close to the building, with instructions to follow down the creek, and when out of sight from the ranch, hurry to Beaver and summon assistance. Concealed by the bushes which grew on the creek bottom, they made good their escape and reached Beaver. Here a company of mounted men, under command of John R. Murdock, was hastily collected, and within one hour after the arrival of the children these men were at Lee's Ranch.

The Indians, discouraged by the gallant defense made by Lee, after making an unsuccessful attack on the ranch house from all sides, took the stock which was convenient and fled. They were followed to a point near the Pah-reab, but made good their escape. None of the people at the ranch were injured except Joseph Lillywhite, whose wound proved to be very serious, but he finally recovered.

It was afterwards learned that two of the Indians killed in this battle were the sons of Timpe-nam-pats. He and his sons had kept their pledge, but it had cost them their lives.

Not Ashamed

The men and the boys who are needed today
Are those not ashamed of the fact that they pray.
Not ashamed, having eyes to admit they behold
Things prophets both ancient and modern have told.
Having ears, not ashamed that they listen and hear
The voice, still and small, but convincing and clear,
Which leads in the way that is narrow and straight,
To life everlasting through Heaven's free gate.

The boy or the man not ashamed to decline
Tobacco and stimulant "out of his line;"
As things quite offensive to mother and wife,
As harmful, indeed, in any man's life,
Unwholesome, injurious, well understood
The word of the Lord has condemned as not good!
My boy, be the one not ashamed, nor afraid,
The true cause of wisdom and honor to aid.

"Unpopular?" Yes, my dear boy, so was He
Who walked on the waves of the blue Galilee;
Yet, God-like and pure, with supreme power filled,
The wind and the waves at His bidding were stilled.
We all need the touch of that power divine,
His spirit to guide us and keep us in line.
May we, while with fervor His love is proclaimed,
So live that of us He will not be ashamed.

                              L. Lula Greene Richards.

His Word of Honor

By *Elsie Chamberlain Carroll*

Dan Schapper was one of the twenty men granted a Thanksgiving parole by Warden Oswold as a test for the new honor system being tried out in the Ridgeford prison.

Dan was serving a five year sentence for attempting to appropriate funds from the Riverdale bank three years before.

This fact had been blazoned to the world by eager newspapers. As usual, the newspapers had failed to make any note of the peculiar subtleness of the temptation which had caused the young man's downfall.

It must take a deal of courage for a man to keep his mind sane and his spirit clear when compelled to forfeit five good years of his life in payment for the weakness of a half hour. This thought often came to Dan in a surge of overwhelming bitterness in those first days within the great wall. He recognized his wrong, but the punishment seemed so out of relation to the crime. And after all, was not the deepest punishment he could ever feel his own remorse when he had realized his crime? This punishment had been made all the keener by Mary's unfaltering love and confidence in his future.

"I believe the prisons make more criminals than they cure," Dan had confided once in a letter to Mary. "But I'm trying hard not to let them make one of me."

Perhaps more than anything else the sweet courage and trust in Mary's letters helped him in this resolve. She never preached or moralized. Principally, her letters told all the intimate details about the little farm they had bought together, and which now she ran alone with the assistance of her fifteen year old nephew, Ben, and about the wonderful growth and development of their baby boy whom he had never seen. (Danny was born three months after the father had been sentenced.) No, Mary did not preach, but there was always something about her letters which made Dan feel that life was worth while after all, and that the future was worth waiting for. And now as a reward for his efforts to keep his resolve, he was to have forty-eight precious hours at home with Mary and the baby.

It was six o'clock on the evening before Thanksgiving when Dan got off the interurban train at the little station a quarter

of a mile from the farm. His eyes were bright and his cheeks
flushed as he started through the familiar fields. He thrilled
with mingled joy and pain at the sight of each dear familiar ob-
ject. How good it was to be treading his own land! He tried
to shut out the realization that this wondrous joy was to be of
such short duration.

Ben had gone to town to spend Thanksgiving with his
mother and sisters, so Mary and little Danny were alone to welcome. the homecomer. It would be hard to depict the joy of
that reunion. All the yearning hunger of three long years must
be appeased in one short day. And yet, Dan and Mary were
thankful for even that brief happiness. At first their hearts
were too full for words. They could only stand with clasped
hands and misty eyes, in glad realization that they were together once more.

Then came the touching introduction of the father and
the little son. The baby's natural shyness and the father's first
real overwhelming sense of fatherhood. Dan had thought he
had realized it before, but now he sensed it first in all its
sacred fulness with the touch of the baby form against his breast.
Mary watched the growing acquaintance with anxious eyes. She
knew the influence of this hour would be great in both the life
of the man and that of the little boy.

As if by mutual consent, both Dan and Mary refrained from
letting the thought of their coming separation mar the bliss
of the present. They would live in the present alone, for this
one day, and make it a thanksgiving day in very deed, yield-
ing to them its maximum of joy.

And so, during that first evening and all through the next
day they laughed and talked and played, trying to forget there
was a morrow.

In the afternoon of Thanksgiving day they took a long
walk over the farm. Little Danny kept his father busy listening
to the wonderful things they would do together, when Jack
Frost went away and they could plant the gardens again. Mary
knew how the child's words must be wrenching the man's heart,
but Dan made no sign.

After supper Dan and the baby had a long romp in the
living room, then the father undressed the tired little fellow and
carried him into bed.

"I's glad you'se comed home," Danny confided as the father
knelt beside the little white bed and held a pair of chubby
hands. "Mama an' Danny won't be lonesome now." He sighed
happily and closed two sleepy eyes. A lump came into the
father's throat. Ought he to break the child's illusion. At
seven o'clock in the morning the train would carry him back
to the prison walls. Danny would wake up and ask for him.

in our youthful memories, until our turn came round. With what disgust did Uncle Phil Margetts or Thomas Ellerbeck, or Joe Simmons, or their wives, yield up their acquisitions! How our father chuckled as he saw his hopefuls vanquish his guests! With what impatience was the game suspended, while mother or aunt borrowed the lamp from the table long enough to hurry into the kitchen to see "what was burning;" and then when the refreshments were passed around with what eagerness did the juveniles sit and listen to their elders discuss the books or poems from which the famous quotations of the evening were derived— or the play—(many of the participants in our circle were members of the noted theatre stock company) from which the sentiments had been selected! These discussions, with the accompanying analyses of quotations, impressed the latter upon the memory of the youthful listeners in an indelible fashion, as nothing else could have done.

I well remember my father's particular favorites among the old adages. Some of them were: "Man proposes but God disposes," *Thomas a' Kempis;* "There's many a slip 'twixt the cup and the lip," *Hazlett;* "There is a divinity which shapes our ends, rough hew them how we will," *Shakespeare;* and "The best laid schemes of mice and men gang aft aglee," *Robert Burns.* Four great minds at different times, had had much the same thought, our father used to say, but all expressed it differently. He particularly loved Robert Burns, and he took pains to explain to his youngsters the meaning of that phrase, "The best laid schemes of mice and men gang aft aglee"—that it was simply another name for disappointment, and that in our lives it is the unexpected that always happens. As time went by the old adage came gradually to be changed to "The best laid *plans* of mice and men gang aft aglee," and that is the way it is generally mis-quoted by the world today. Some time afterward, our own little circle had the force of the saying impressed upon us. My brother, Orson F. Whitney, well known to all of you, had an overwhelming ambition in his early youth, to become an actor. All his studies were bent to that end, and under Dr. John R. Park, at the old Univeristy of Deseret, he attained high proficiency as a reciter and school boy orator. No Friday afternoon's special exercise in the old Council House, then located on the *Deseret News* corner of today, was complete without a recitation from him, or a dramatic sketch in which he was the principal player. At last, when he was about twenty years of age, came the climax. He made up his mind to leave for the east, and armed himself with letters of introduction from theatrical folk here, to managers and actors in New York. The Wasatch Literary Society, of which he was one of the founders, gave him a farewell benefit in the Social Hall. It was a rare event. All the amateur talent of the city took part, and a goodly purse was realized. My brother was jubilant. Next morning an envelope, marked Box B, arrived at his home. Opening it, he found it contained a call for a mission to the eastern states, signed by Brigham Young. It was probably his first great trial, but he answered the call, and changed the whole course of his life. I fancy I can see the twinkle in my father's eye as he murmured, "The best laid plans of mice and men gang aft aglee." I am not sure, at this distance, that this may not have been the guiding hand that sent those plans "ganging aft." Either his, or that of the bishop's mother, a deeply religious woman, who did not sympathize with the stage aspirations of her son. In any event, but for that change there would have been no Bishop Whitney of the 18th Ward, no Church historian or poet, and no Apostle Whitney of today. I think he himself learned to feel that "there is a divinity which shapes our ends, rough hew them how we will."

Speaking of that particular saying and of Dr. Park, recalls that he, too, was a great lover of the literary masters, and in his classes of rhetoric or grammar, he made it a rule to give out a quotation which some student would be called on to write on the blackboard and analyze. One day he read that sentiment, "There is a divinity which shapes our ends, rough hew them how we will." A tall somewhat bashful boy from the country, was called to the board. He looked a little troubled and uncertain, but finally he wrote out in clear characters, "There is a divinity which *shakes* our ends——" He got no further. Dr. Park himself led in the roars of laughter which followed, and the boy in bewilderment went back to his seat. I had forgotten who the boy was until years afterward; in company, one evening, the story was told, and Prof. Horace H. Cummings, the present able head of the Church educational system, said he could vouch for the yarn because the boy at the blackboard was himself.

Dr. Park himself was an illustration of the truth of the saying he loved to quote. He, the father of our great University, and the first to hold the office of superintendent of education under statehood, started life in a small way as a doctor, in Tiffin, Ohio. He was practicing medicine when the call of the Civil War came, and he joined the Union army. To be a successful surgeon was his highest ambition. Who could have dreamed that the end of the war would send him to Utah where he attained one of the highest positions within the gift of the state! In a few weeks, we shall all unite at the University he founded, in dedicating the great Administration Building and giving it his name, later erecting within its walls a majestic bronze statue in his memory.

The pages of history are crowded with instances of great

sire. But still more do I desire the approval of one man, and his name is James A. Garfield."

The great McKinley, famous as the author of the tariff bill which bears his name, was once a school teacher at $25 a month, and if he ever thought of the presidential chair, it must have seemed very remote to him. He was distinguished as one of the purest minded and ablest presidents of our later days. He, too, fell before the bullet of an assassin, the fanatic Czolgosz. His death was as impressive as his life. His last words were, "Goodbye, all, goodbye. It is God's. way. His will, not ours, be done." Truly it might be said of this Christian president, as it was of Addison:

> "He taught us how to live, and oh, too high
> The price of knowledge; he taught us how to die."

In the youth of Lincoln, the first of the martyred presidents, the gap that separated him from the presidency, probably seemed wider than that spanned by any who reached the position before or since. He began life as a rail splitter but the axe he wielded blazed his way to immortality.

I recently read a new account of the assassination of President Lincoln, which may interest some of my youthful hearers. As you all know, he was killed in Ford's Theatre, Washington, by an actor, J. W. Booth, during a performance of "Our American Cousin." A committee, knowing the president would attend the theatre that night, decorated his box with the Stars and Stripes. A discussion took place as to whether the flag should be draped on the box below or overhead. It was decided that it should be hung over the front rail, and it was this little fact that led to the capture of the assassin. He stealthily entered the president's box at the back, and shot him from behind, he immediately placed his foot on the ledge of the box, and prepared to leap to the stage, but he wore a spur and this caught on the flag drapery on the box, causing him to trip, so that when he fell on the stage, his ankle was broken. This made it impossible for him to retreat rapidly, so that by the time he reached the back door and leaped on the back of his waiting horse, his pursuers were already upon his track and he was traced to a deserted barn, where he was shot to death a day or two later. Thus, the narrator impressively observed, the flag, to which he was a traitor, became the avenging agency which brought the murderer to his doom.

And now, to conclude, let us ask what is the lesson to be drawn from these instances I have cited? Simply this, and it is the thought I would leave with you—that our lives are not the result of accident, that the great Architect of the Universe leaves nothing to chance. Every son and daughter of God, from the loftiest to the least, came upon the earth for a purpose, and being here they are the creatures of their Father's care until they are summoned back into his presence. He holds us in the hollow of his hand, and even the hairs upon our heads are numbered. Victor Hugo, in his wonderful picture of Napoleon, describing how that great conqueror's mighty plans went "aft aglee," said: "It was not possible that Napoleon should win at Waterloo. Why? Because of Wellington? No. Because of Blucher? No. Because of Grouchy? No; because of God!" And the thought of Napoleon recalls that other broken figure in the tragedy of all the ages, the German Kaiser. What must be his thoughts, as he broods in his exile at Amerongen today, and views all the wreck that lies behind, to say nothing of the spectres that stand before him! Only a brief twelve months ago, he was at the head of a mighty host, seemingly invincible, advancing upon the French and English armies and rolling them back upon Paris and the English channel as a giant's hand might roll up a scroll; the whole world held its breath, and we all felt the chill of apprehension, when the boaster issued his invitations to the journalists and historians of his own and the neutral countries to march with his armies into the French capitol. But in his boastful reckonings he forgot one thing— America. At the last hour of what seemed the last day, when France and England were staggering and all civilization seemed to totter, the armies of America planted themselves before the on-rushing Huns, and formed the rock upon which they "foamed themselves away." Once more the hand of Divinity was made manifest. Truly we might echo the thought of Hugo and say: It was not possible that Germany should triumph in this conflict. Why? Because of Foch? No. Because of Pershing? No; because of God!

Home a Basis of Peace

Home is a basis of peace, because when it succeeds, it cultivates the germ elements of peace, that sprout and grow in every home-built heart of mankind, until finally a great world peace garden will flourish. These precious germ elements are not only the social agents of life, liberty and happiness, but they are the force of all spiritual developments as well. The home that is to have influence in establishing world peace, must make itself a model of permanency and love: a brother, a sister, a wife, a husband, a father, a mother, these are our nearest neighbors. If the law of love is not made to work with them, what shall we expect when it is applied to a fellow townsman, not to mention an enemy in Europe.   *G. Gilbert Meldrum.*

The Mormon Battalion

To the land of fair promise, the glorious West,
They came with the flag that their fathers had blest.
And there, on the shore of the great peaceful Sea,
They planted this flag of the brave and the free.

Over mountain and valley and desert and plain,
They built the great highway that reached to the main;
And with girdles of iron and rivets of gold
They welded the East and West in one fold.

They flung open the doors, and the wonders revealed
Of the vaults of the ages, long hidden and sealed;
And into the lap of the nation was rolled
The wealth of their treasure, unreckoned, untold.

By a touch that was magic, they scattered in rills
The streams that rushed down from the snow-crested hills;
And the valleys beneath, that were barren and gray,
Were transfigured with beauty in wondrous array.

It was not theirs to know what their labors had wrought,
Though they served with a fulness of purpose and thought.
It was not theirs to reap, though the seeds that were sown
Fell in rich, fertile soil and in beauty have grown.

For us is the harvest. We carner the store;
And they who come after shall garner still more,
For the empire they founded was not for a day,
But in majesty rises as years pass away.

On the hillside they rest, 'neath the green, waving grass,
Where the blossoms bend low as the Wasatch winds pass.
They are resting. The work of our heroes is done;
They have been mustered out and called home one by one.

And the future shall write them in bronze and in stone—
Their name and their day and the deeds they have done;
And the youth of the land who beholds it and reads
Shall read life's greatest lesson—the lesson of deeds.

May Belle T. Davis.

ELDER JOSEPH W. McMURRIN
*Of the First Council of Seventy, recently appointed President of the
California Mission.*

Mission Leaders

By *Edward H. Anderson*

President Joseph W. McMurrin

Elder Joseph W. McMurrin, who recently took charge of
the California mission, was born September 5, 1858, in Tooele
city, Utah. His parents, Joseph McMurrin, and Margaret Lean-
ing McMurrin, arrived in Salt Lake City, during the early winter of 1856, moving thence to Tooele and later returning to Salt
Lake City while Joseph was still a young child. He has since continued to reside in Salt Lake City all his life, except such times
as he has been absent upon missions.

He received his education in the public schools of Salt Lake
City, and in his boyhood and young manhood his time was occupied as a teamster, freighting ore from the mining camps of
Ophir, Bingham, and Park City, and hauling in return, wood or
coal to Salt Lake City. He was also later employed by the City
of Salt Lake, in assisting to establish a city water system.

As a stone cutter he assisted in preparing blocks of granite
for the walls of the Salt Lake temple, for about two years, and
for several years was engaged as receipting clerk in the Bishop's
storehouse.

On the first of February, 1876, before he was eighteen years
of age, he was called on a mission to Arizona, to aid in colo-
nizing the locality, and assisted as one of the pioneers in found-
ing the little settlement of St. Joseph, on the Little Colorado
river. This settlement was established by about fifty men under the presidency of William C. Allen, now a patriarch in the
Jordan stake. After spending two years in building canals,
dams, and hauling logs and building log houses, plowing, plant-
ing, lumbering, and doing other lines of work incident to pioneer life, he returned to Salt Lake City, expecting to find a wife,
expecting later to return to Arizona and make a permanent
home. However, shortly after his return, he was released from
the Arizona mission and called to Great Britain.

In October, 1881, he left for his first European mission, being assigned to Scotland. He presided over the Scottish mission
for at least seven months of his term, returning home in November, 1883. During this mission he baptized fifty persons, among
them being two of his father's sisters.

During the "raid," in 1885, he came near losing his life,

being shot twice in the bowels by a United States deputy marshal. The bullets passed entirely through his body. A remarkable miracle occurred in his healing. Being shot or wounded in such a vital part, no hope was entertained that human skill could be of any avail in saving his life. The most eminent doctors of the city were positive in their opinon that he could not live, says his biographer, Edwin F. Parry. He himself felt that his life was fast ebbing away, and he fully expected to die. While in this condition, he was visited by Elder John Henry Smith, of the Council of the Twelve, to whom he related what the doctors had told him, and expressed his own belief in the correctness of their views. After hearing his story, Elder Smith took him by the hand and said: "Brother Joseph, as an apostle of the Lord Jesus, I promise you, in the name of Jesus Christ, that if you desire to live you shall live, no matter what doctors may say to you to the contrary." The Lord heard the promise, and in his merciful kindness, fulfilled the prediction of his inspired servant, and spared the life of Brother McMurrin. The wounds were healed, and Elder McMurrin was completely restored to soundness of body. His recovery was a miracle, wrought by the power of the Lord, and he freely and emphatically acknowledges that such was the case.

In July, 1886, Elder McMurrin departed for a second European mission, laboring twenty months in the Bristol conference, and twenty-eight months in the London conference, in which he presided for twenty-six months. His wife accompanied him, and a son and daughter were born to them while on this mission.

For a third mission to Europe, he left home in July, 1896, and returned in December, 1898, during which time he was one of the presidency of the mission, with Rulon S. Wells, and traveled extensively through all the countries embraced in the European mission, in which the elders were conducting work at the time, and also in some nations where no missionaries were located, such as France, Austria and Italy. It was while he was in Liverpool on this mission that he was chosen, at the October conference, 1897, a member of the First Council of Seventy, being ordained and set apart for the position by President Anthon H. Lund, in Liverpool, January 21, 1898, when President Lund passed through Liverpool *en route* to the Holy Land, on a mission assigned him by the Presidency of the Church.

In 1901-2, Elder McMurrin filled a short mission to Boise, Idaho, in company with Elder Melvin J. Ballard, at which time he aided in the organization of the Boise branch of the Church, which branch continued to be a strong one until the Boise stake was organized, when it became the headquarters of that stake of Zion.

In the interim between his missions, he served as a home

missionary in the old Salt Lake stake, from 1883 to 1886, and from 1890 to 1896. For several years he has been a member of the Y. M. M. I. A. General board, the Religion Class board, and the General Priesthood committee. He was associated with the late Elder A. O. Woodruff in establishing the first colony sent to the Big Horn country, and assisted him in the organization of the Big Horn stake, suggesting the name of Byron for one of the two towns that were first laid out in the stake, being in honor of Byron Sessions, first president of the stake.

For the past twenty-two years, Elder McMurrin has been active in visiting the stakes of Zion in company with members of the Council of the Twelve apostles, and laboring among the Seventies, Mutual Improvement organizations, Religion classes, and in other directions, as called upon by the authorities. Elder Mc-Murrin is a man of wonderful spirituality, strong in the faith, with an unflinching testimony of the divinity of the work of the Lord established by the Prophet Joseph Smith. His earnest and simple testimonies of the goodness of God to him, and the power accompanying the administration of the servants of the Lord, never fail to touch the hearts of the people who hear. He possesses remarkable discretion and discernment. His studious habits, his willingness to obey counsel, and his full and large experience in the practical matters of the Church and of life, specially qualify him for leadership in his new calling, and his thousands of friends wish him the success that is sure to come as a reward of his earnestness and faith in the cause of the Lord.

Bishop Heber C. Iverson

As previously mentioned in the *Era*, Elder Melvin J. Ballard, for many years president of the Northwestern States mission, was recently ordained an apostle, and is now a member of the Council of the Twelve, and has therefore been released as president of the Northwestern States mission.

Bishop Heber C. Iverson, of the Second ward, Salt Lake City, Liberty stake of Zion, was chosen to fill the vacancy. Bishop Iverson received official notice of his appointment in a letter from the First Presidency, dated March 9, 1919, and left for his new field of labor on April 14, having been set apart for the position on the 6th day of April.

Bishop Iverson was born in Salt Lake City, Utah, July 1, 1868, and has resided in Salt Lake City, all his life. His father's name of Soren Iverson, and his mother's Caroline Monson. His parents came to Utah in October, 1854. He received his education in the district schools of Salt Lake City, in the Salt Lake Stake academy, and in the Latter-day Saints college, of which latter he is a graduate.

In 1891, Bishop Iverson went on a mission to Arizona and New Mexico for the Y. M. M. I. A. He also filled a mission to the Southern States, leaving home on June 24, 1893. Owing to his father's death, he returned in March, 1895. Prior to his leaving for this mission, on December 28, 1892, he was married to Anna B. Erickson, and they have six children. Lieut. Heber Frank, who lately returned from Camp Taylor, Orabelle, Joseph Grant, Owen, Paul and Preston. The whole family is expecting to join him in Oregon, in June. He has filled practically every position in the priesthood, and in the auxiliary organizations of the ward, having been secretary of the deacons, president of the home missionaries, secretary and counselor and president of the Y. M. M. I. A.; stake aid to Superintendent Joseph H. Felt in the Y. M. M. I. A. of the Salt Lake stake, when the whole county belonged to one stake. He was also counselor to Richard R. Lyman, of the Council of the Twelve, then superintendent of the Y. M. M. I. A. of the Salt Lake stake. He has been also Sunday School teacher and assistant superintendent. On June 24, 1899, the same date that he left for his mission in 1893, he was set apart as bishop of the Second ward, Liberty stake, a position that he held until his call to the new presidency of the Northwestern States mission. Since he was appointed bishop, he has missed being out to speak on Sundays before some gathering or other only three or four Sundays in all those years, being regularly called by various organizations. He is a fluent speaker, and well versed in the scriptures, and in the doctrines of the gospel.

Besides his proficiency in ecclesiastical and religious affairs, he is efficient and prominent in business, having labored

BISHOP HEBER C. IVERSON

Successor to Elder Melvin J. Ballard of the Council of the Twelve, as President of Northwestern States Mission.

in the wholesale grocery department of the Z. C. M. I. since 1897, all these years. For years he has been interested in active work in civic government. Among other duties, he has been a prominent member of the central committee for the old folks entertainment, a movement characteristic of the Latter-day Saints, showing forth their interest in and care for the aged. Bishop Iverson has a wide acquaintance throughout the Church. He is well posted in theological matters, and is an earnest and powerful public speaker. We join his many friends in wishing him success in his new calling.

Nephi Jensen

The twenty-second mission district of the Church of Jesus Christ of Latter-day Saints is shortly to be opened in Eastern Canada, and is to be presided over by Elder Nephi Jensen, a former missionary in the Southern States, and now a practicing attorney in Salt Lake City. The district or section of country composing this conference was formerly a part of the Eastern States mission. The headquarters have not yet been selected, but will doubtless be located in some eastern Canadian city. The twenty-one missions heretofore established in different parts of the world are: Australia, Britain, California, Central States, Eastern States, Hawaii, Japan, Mexico, Netherlands, New Zealand, Northern States, Northwestern States, Samoa, Scandinavia, Southern States, South Africa, Swiss and German, Swedish, Tahitian, Tongan, and Western States; the twenty-second mission, Canada, will shortly be organized, as stated.

NEPHI JENSEN

President of the new Canadian Mission.

Elder Jensen, is the eighth new mission head recently appointed in the different missions. Nephi Jensen was born February 16, 1876, in Salt Lake City, Utah. He attended the public schools in Sugar House. His parents later moved to Montezuma county, Colorado, where he attended the high school one year. His schooling was further continued at the Latter-day Saints college, Salt Lake City, and later at the summer school, at the University of Utah, where he attended in the early part of 1905. In February, 1898, he was sent on his first mission to the Southern States, where he labored with diligence and success until June, 1900, when he returned home.

In the spring of 1907, he left to fill a second mission to the Southern States, serving, at that time, as secretary of the mission, until November, 1908. Following and during his mission labors, he passed the studies of the senior year in the law department of the University of Chattanooga, where he received the degree of LL. B., in the class of 1908. He had, however, been admitted to the bar of the Supreme Court of Utah, February, 1906. He served as a member of the Utah State Legislature, during the term beginning November, 1906.

After his return from his first mission to the Southern States, he married Margaret Smith, a daughter of the late Jesse N. Smith, on April 9, 1902. They have one son, Paul, age seven years. Elder Jensen taught school for five years, from 1901 to 1906. In January, 1909, he continued the practice of law in Salt Lake City, which he has been engaged in up to the present time. He acted as Assistant County Attorney of Salt Lake county, from January, 1911, to August, 1913. In recent years, he has been a member of the Council of the 105th quorum of Seventy, and a home missionary in the Granite stake of Zion, where he has made many friends. His ability as a speaker, and his diligence in the service of the Church, is recognized by all who have heard and known him. He has contributed largely to home publications, and readers of the *Improvement Era* are not unfamiliar with his writings, his recent eulogy of President Joseph F. Smith having especially attracted attention. His many friends feel sure that he will make good in the honor that has come to him to found a new mission of the Church.

Tolerance

My friend that was, I cast away—
  He'd many faults that gave me pain!
But his heart comes singing back today:
  "God made none without blot or stain,
Why, 'tis the sun that casts the shade,
  The one we love best gives most fears;
Of gall and honey life is made,
  And eyes that smile, also shed tears."

G. G. *Meldrum.*

The League of Nations

By *Hon. Carl A. Badger*

In an address on "International Peace," before the Nobel Prize committee, delivered at Christiania, Norway, May 5, 1910, Theodore Roosevelt, in outlining the means by which the cause of international peace among nations should be advanced, suggested:

First, further treaties of arbitration; second, further development of The Hague tribunal and of the work of the conference and court of The Hague; third, "something should be done as soon as possible to check the growth of armaments, especially naval armaments, by international agreement;" fourth, and "finally, it would be a master stroke if those great powers honestly bent on peace would form a league of peace, not only to keep the peace, among themselves, but to prevent, by force if necessary, its being broken by others." The weakness of the work done by The Hague arose, in his opinion, "from the lack of an executive power, of any police power, to enforce the decrees of the court."

We are denied the advice and counsel of this great statesman, as far as the concrete proposal is concerned for the enforcement of peace emanating from the conference now in session at Paris, but we may reasonably believe that had he lived he would have been an earnest advocate of the league, and would have given to the proposal that constructive and friendly criticism necessary for its successful establishment and the accomplishment of its great aims. There are but few dissenting voices in the great chorus of hope and prayers for the success of the present serious and determined effort on the part of civilized nations, to interpose obstacles in the path of those who believe that war is necessary or desirable and to offer an escape to those nations that look upon war as necessary only because no means has yet been provided for peaceful solution of international difficulties consistent with honor and a maintenance of international rights.

The proposed league will manifest its principal activities through the following agencies:

1. An executive council, composed of the representatives of nine nations.
2. An assembly of delegates composed of representatives from all nations belonging to the league.

3. A judicial tribunal for the adjudication of legal questions.

4. An expert military and naval commission to advise on a program of limitation of armaments and to watch and secure the observance of such program, when agreed to by the nations, and to advise the military assistance necessary to be contributed by the nations who are members of the league, in case it becomes necessary to vindicate by force the covenants of the league.

5. A permanent secretariat, consisting of a secretary with a force of clerical assistants to keep the records of the league and its various administrative, consultative, and judicial bodies, and with whom all treaties between the nations who are members of the league must be registered and published before they become binding.

6. A mandate commission which will investigate and inspect and report to the league the conduct of the nations to whom are entrusted the responsibility and obligation of supervising and assisting backward nations, liberated by the great war, principally German colonies and submerged peoples heretofore under Turkish dominion.

7. A labor bureau which shall investigate the conditions of labor throughout the world and shall propose measures for the improvement of the condition of those who toil.

The executive council is one of the most important, if not the most important, of all of the agencies of the league. The great nations who have won the war, the United States of America, the British Empire, France, Italy and Japan, will each have permanent representatives on this council, and a minority representation of four will be selected by the assembly of delegates from among the other nations that belong to the league. The executive council must meet at least once a year. The first meeting of the council as well as the first meeting of the assembly, is to be called by the President of the United States. Matters within the jurisdiction of the executive council may be referred to the assembly in case the executive council desires the advice and the benefit of the more general discussion and consideration possible in the larger assembly, and in case of disputes properly coming before the executive council for investigation, parties to the dispute may, within a limited time, elect to transfer the matter to the assembly for its determination.

The great benefit that will arise from the League of Nations will flow, it is anticipated, largely out of the fact that it will be possible for the nations to regularly and periodically come together for the discussion of the matters which concern world peace and welfare. One of the difficulties with The Hague has been that while great good has arisen from its conferences, the meetings were not fixed for definite time and our minister to the Netherlands, Dr. Henry Van Dyke, to whom was entrusted the duty of initiating a movement for another meeting at The Hague, found his efforts frustrated and blocked by Germany and the nations who sympathized and worked with her. It is said by experienced statesmen, that if Sir Edward Gray, British secretary of state for foreign affairs, in his efforts to find a peaceful solution of the Serbian-Austrian situation, had been successful in his attempt to compel Germany to enter a conference with the other European nations in July, 1914, Germany could not have gone to war. A peaceful way out of the difficulty would have been found, if a meeting had been brought about. Germany knew this and would not meet.

The greatest interest in the workings of the league center around its handling of questions of war and peace, though it is by no means certain that this will be true in the distant future. War between nations may then be as unlikely as personal encounter between individuals today. International law and world conscience may restrain lawless propensities of nations, just as private law restrains the individual within nations today; firmly established law and adequate force are indispensable to any such accomplishment.

As an obstacle to war, it is provided that no nation belonging to the league shall go to war without submitting the matter in dispute to arbitration before a tribunal selected by the parties to the dispute; for example, a tribunal such as was organized specially for the determination of the controversy between Great Britain and the United States, with reference to the seals in Alaskan waters, or to a permanent tribunal such as The Hague, to which were submitted our differences with Mexico over the so-called "Pious Fund," or to the judicial tribunal created by the league, or if it is found impossible for the disputants to submit the matter to judicial determination, that then, at least, it shall be submitted to the executive council or, if desired, to the assembly of delegates for an investigation of its merits; and if the investigation results in a unanimous decision, it is agreed that the members of the league shall not go to war against a party submitting to the decision or if the matter is arbitrated to the award of the arbitrators. The members of the league further agree that in any event they will not go to war until three months after the decision or award. The difference between matters which may be submitted to judicial determination and those which may only be submitted to investigation and recommendation would follow the general distinction between so-called "justiciable" and "non-justiciable" questions. The first includes such matters as an interpretation of a law or treaty or a question of fact, such as a boundary. The latter concerns matters which affect honor and sovereignty of nations and which, while everybody admits they exist, are very difficult of exact definition. The distinction has been drawn, with his usual masterly ability, by Senator Root, in his great letter in support of the league, as follows:

"Disputes of a justiciable character are defined as disputes as to the interpretation of a treaty, as to any question of international law, as to the existence of any fact which if established would constitute a breach of any international obligation, or as to the nature and extent of the reparation · to be made for any such breach."

This definition is embodied in the revised compact of the league, as announced by the press of April 28. It is also provided that before conflict arises, each nation shall have the friendly right to suggest to the executive council that a matter likely to produce difficulty, or lead to war, has arisen, or is about to arise between any of the nations. It is further provided that in case of serious dispute between nations not members of the league or between a nation which is a member and one which is not a member of the league that the non-member nation or nations shall be invited to become members of the league for the purpose of settlement of the difficulty. In case any nation shall go to war without submitting the matter to arbitration or investigation, the members of the league agree that they will sever all intercourse, political, commercial and personal, and will isolate such nation. Germany and her allies have been whipped in the present conflict largely through commercial and material pressure. This is a powerful weapon, and one which will become all the more powerful as the interdependence between nations further develops.

It is agreed that the executive council shall formulate and recommend to the nations a program for limitation of armaments. The great burden in taxation imposed upon the people because of the competition between nations in the equipping of armies and building of navies, as well as the actual provocation to war and the facility to conflict which exists in a large professional army fully equipped and ready for conflict, is recognized by all. It is agreed that after the program of limitation of armament has been accepted by the nations composing the league that they will not thereafter increase their armament without the consent of the executive council.

It is urged that an agreement of this kind would be in derogation of our sovereignty, and that we would be placing in the hands of "foreigners" the determination of the size of our army and navy, and that such a provision would be unconstitutional. It will be noted that Senator Root, in his letter regarding the proposed constitution for the league, has not suggested a single consitutional objection to the covenant. This is a fairly safe indication that none exists. It is, humanly speaking, certain that if any had existed, it would not have escaped his keen, informed and practiced intellect. Ex-President Taft, who is also a great lawyer and experienced judge, has expressly annouced his opinion that there is nothing opposed to the constitution of the United States in the covenant of the league. For more than one hundred years we have had an agreement with Canada doing away with the necessity of military establishments along the boundary between the two nations and the maintenance of war ships on the Great Lakes. No one has suggested that this agreement is unconstitutional. This provision of the constitution of the proposed league would not differ in principle from our agreement with Canada, but would apply the principle of limitation of armaments now in operation with Canada to all the nations composing the league. The league only "recommends" the program. To be binding on the United States, the recommendation would have to be approved by Congress. The only question is as to the policy of such an agreement, and as to this particular matter it would seem that any program of disarmament likely to succeed must be one entered into by all nations. This is necessary because of the fact that no nation can determine its policy in the matter of disarmaments until all of the other nations have made a determination of theirs. The determination must, as a practical matter, be arrived at at the same time among all nations.

As a result of the war there have been liberated from German and Turkish dominion great tracts of land in Africa and Asia and in the islands of the Pacific. The question of the disposition of these lands is a serious one. The people are backward in development, and it would seem unfair and unwise to turn them adrift. It would be wrong to place them back in the hands of Germany; she has demonstrated her unfitness to govern other peoples. The league has proposed to take these peoples and lands under its jurisdiction as a trust to promote their civilization, and welfare; and it has agreed that the more advanced nations shall be selected as mandatories, or "big brothers," to assist in bringing these peoples up to a standard of civilization. The most urgent need of these nations is law and order and assistance in procuring food. It has been suggested that the United States act as mandate for Armenia or Palestine. It is provided in the league that the consent of the mandatory must be secured, so that the matter is in no sense compulsory. If we undertake this responsibility it will be because we decide that we ought to. The new spirit with reference to colonies is that they are not to be exploited or tyrannized over, but are to be helped along the road of civilization and world pro ress.

Article X provides that the members of the league "shall undertake to respect and preserve, as against external aggression, the territorial integrity and existing political independence of all states members of the league." This has been attacked as binding us to enter into any conflict that may arise in the "far flung" British empire, or to oppose, or it may be to forcibly suppress, any effort on the part of Ireland to free itself from Great

Britain. Senator Root in his declaration with regard to the league, has said that after mature consideration and after some doubt as to its wisdom, he is in favor of Article X. Many new states are being created out of the nations defeated in the great war, among them Poland, Czecho-Slovakia and Jugo-Slavia. Their existence is dependent upon the friendly assistant of the great nations that have made victory possible, and upon the threat of the use of the strength of these nations, if necessary, to protect the new nations. It will be noticed that the obligation is to protect only against "external aggression." This would clearly not include any effort on the part of Ireland to free itself. The aim of the article is unquestionably only against the land-grabbing propensities of the old order. We guaranteed the new independence of New Granada in 1846, of Panama in 1903, and of Haiti, in 1916. The principle is not new, it is simply an application with geographical extension of an old principle to a new world condition.

Any objection to Article X seems to lose its force in face of the fact that a nation may withdraw from the league by giving two years' notice. If we find ourselves bound to the discharge of undesirable obligations, we may withdraw.

When we think of the great benefits that may possibly, indeed that will in all likelihood, flow from this effort on the part of mankind to free itself from the necessity of unnecessary wars, the instincts of humanity, faith in the possibility of human progress and in the strength of an overruling Providence, seem to concur in the prayer that man may be successful in this beneficent undertaking. No greater political question was ever presented to human mind for solution. We are each of us a factor in world opinion, and we owe it to ourselves and to the future that we carefully consider this great question, and bring our voice and influence to the side which conscience and reason and faith commends to be the right side.

We live by faith and not by sight. Difference of opinion as to the possibilities of success of the proposed league is not to be wondered at. Patrick Henry opposed the adoption of the constitution of the United States. His argument against the constitution is interesting reading. He had with him some of the most patriotic and capable men of his day. We, today, regard the constitution as divinely inspired, and Gladstone has characterized it as the greatest product of the human mind stricken off in a given time. We refused for twenty years to ratify the Geneva Convention establishing the Red Cross, because it was thought to violate our traditional policy against "entangling alliances." It is well that there are those who doubt and question. Doubt and criticism test the soundness of the project, but, after all, sane and courageous faith is the safer guide. Let us trust "the soul's invincible surmise," and believe that it is possible for men to effectuate his highest aspirations for an honorable and practical means of achieving peace.

As we stand in the presence of the four years of terrible struggle and doubt now past, and see clearly the vindication of right and justice and the signal defeat and punishment of wrong, let us renew our faith in God and in the reign of law among nations. Let faith live and doubt die. With Lincoln, "Let us have faith that right makes might;" and that right is powerful enough to find a way out of the necessity of the wrong of war.

Nations, like individuals, learn to know and trust each other only by coming closer together. The League of Nations is the next step in human progress. Our honorable part in this establishment is a crowning finish to the tardy but heroic assistance given by us to the upholding of civilization in its hour of direst need.

Salt Lake City, May 1, 1919

O, my Mountains

O, my mountains, how I love you,
   Love your every rise and fall;
And though I wander sea or prairie
   Ever do I hear your call.

Calling me to peace and safety;
   Shelt'ring me from tide and gale.
And your gentle breezes whisp'ring
   Fairy stories, as they sail.

Telling of your wondrous beauty,
   Of your great, majestic power;
How you guide the rushing river,
   How you nurse the daintiest flower.

O, my mountains, yes, I love you,
   Love your every rock and rill;
And, while gazing on your splendor,
   Awake to do the Master's will.
                          Viola Browning.

Memorial Ode

Written for the Dedication of the John R. Park Memorial Building, June 9. 1919

WORDS AND MUSIC BY EVAN STEPHENS.

Ye halls that rise, A firm foundation lies, Of ev er last ing mighty hills be-

neath your walls, Strong and se - cure, Ce ment-ed to en - dure, Thro'

a-ges yet to come, What-er be falls, Thro' a-ges yet to come, What-

glorious shall a - bide Your names to - geth-er blent, be loved and

glorious shall a bide Your names to - geth-er blent, be - loved and

famed, Your names to - geth-er blent, be - loved and famed.

fames, Your names to - geth-er blent, be - loved and famed.

Messages from the Soldiers

[The *Era* has received numerous letters from the soldier boys abroad. Some of these are printed in the certain belief that they will interest our readers, as much as they have entertained the editors. From Prum, Germany, under date of March 21, 1919, Private Alward sends this censored message to the *Era.—Editors.*]

Old Glory at Treves

By *Prvt. S. Alward*

A few days ago I received from a friend two copies of the *Era*, and I certainly was pleased with them. Especially when they were the first copies I have had since coming overseas.

Porta Nigra, Treves, Germany, Formerly Main Entrance to the City.

I have seen many sights since coming to Germany, and those which impress me most of all, are the old Roman structures at Treves (Trier).

Treves is the oldest town in Germany. The town exists

since the reign of Emperor Augustus. In the second half of the third century, when numerous emperors fought each other, the town was often besieged, and at that time was surrounded by strong walls, the Porta Nigra being the main entrance gate.

The river Moselle, which flows through the outskirts of the town was at one time red with blood of martyred Christians, who were ordered killed by Diocletian, and their bodies were then thrown into the river.

The Amphitheatre, a very old historic place, is still visible, showing the animal dens, and the prison cellars where the victims of the wild beasts were kept, and portions of the spectators' galleries. In the Arena thousands of German prisoners were put to death by order of Constantine.

The Kaiserpalace and Roman Baths, built in the early centuries, are very interesting. A number of ancient churches still exist, and have very wonderful traditions. The interior as well as the exterior decorations are very unique. The tombs of many of the old Christian Fathers, and also of a number of local rulers, are in the basements of the churches.

The Church Saint Paulinus was built in commemoration of St. Paulinus, an early Christian bishop, and thousands of Christian martyrs.

The interior decorations of this church are wonderfully clever and magnificent. In the basement, I saw the tombs of the old Burgomaster of Treves, and tombs of three senators, also tombs with thousands of bones of Christian martyrs.

In glass cases on the walls are numerous trimmed and decorated bones of Christians. Treves, at the present time, is quite a progressive business city, with a population of about 65,000. It has a number of up-to-date buildings, and street cars. But the old fashioned, crooked, narrow streets, still exist, notwithstanding a few modern looking streets are to be seen.

Quite a number of American soldiers are stationed at Treves, and the city is visited daily by hundreds of soldiers on leave.

The best sight of all is to see Old Glory floating in the breeze, high above the buildings.

I wish the *Era* success, and will be glad when I can get home, and again read each issue.

From Siberia, Russia

By *Prvt. T. E. Hunsaker, Co. I, 31st Inft., A. E. F., Siberia*

Dear Brother Charles A. Callis and Family, Southern States Mission: No doubt you will be somewhat surprised to hear from me. Since my arrival in the land of Siberia, I have thought of you and the splendid good times we experienced in old Virginia at General conference time; how anxious I was to see them come! And now I am here on another mission. It is impossible for me to explain to you how much I appreciate the knowledge and testimony of the gospel I gained while in your charge as a missionary of truth and righteousness, for it has meant all to me since my experience in army life.

· We have quite a number of "Mormon" boys here, and some who labored in the Southern States.

I have been selected to help preside over the boys, and we meet at every opportunity. The Y. M. C. A. has kindly granted us the use of one of their rooms. The boys are fine, and I testify to you that it is wonderful to note the splendid example they are setting.

Conditions here are much better than one would expect. It is a splendid time for the people to hear the true gospel. We were the first elders to land in this country to my knowledge.

We are very busy here, and from all appearances we shall have to tail the Bolsheviks before they will give in.

I am feeling fine, and being cared for nicely. With kindest regards to all, praying always for your advocacy of truth, your brother in the gospel.

Heroes in Ambulance Service

[The following is an extract under date of March 26, 1919, from an Army paper published at the American Army camp at Brest, France.

It has some interest for Salt Lakers for the reason that a number of our leading citizens, during the month of June, 1917, equipped two ambulances for this service, and a small unit of Salt Lake boys immediately left for the front in France, arriving there in the early part of July.

This unit has now arrived home. The young men who compose the section from Salt Lake and who are now veterans in the service, are: Wallace Julian Burton, Richard Goss, Clifford Davis, and Daniel Spencer, although the latter was separated from the unit last fall, and detailed to another branch of the service.—Editors.]

Men Who Were First Americans to See Service in France Are on Way to States

Original veterans of the American Expeditionary Forces are the men of the United States Ambulance Service, of whom there are ten sections in camp waiting the home-bound transport.

This branch was formed of Americans during the fall of

1914 who, through sympathy with the cause of the poilu, paid their own expenses to Europe to enlist in the French army, recruiting being made through a bureau in Paris.

Three of the sections now in Pontanezen are of this type and they have seen the war from the battle of the Marne to the armistice. The other seven, comprised mostly of university students, entered the service in June, 1917, part of them sailing immediately for the front, and the balance, after a period of training in Allentown, Pa., embarked for France August 20, the same year. They have been on every front from the Swiss border to the North Sea.

There were eighty-seven sections of the United States ambulance service in the field at the armistice, totaling about 4,000 men, under command of Colonel Percy L. Jones, M. C. Twenty-eight per cent of the strength had been cited for valor, and their casualty list is one-third higher than any other American branch.

Because their work has been for the greater part with the French forces, the cock of Verdun was chosen for their shoulder insignia.

The First Utah Field Hospital

By *Sgt. Matthew F. Noall*

[Sgt. Noall, Field Hospital 159, American E. F., Mars la Tour, Meurthe et Moselle, France, has written the following brief history of the First Utah Field Hospital Organization, which he has sent to the *Era* with the approval of the commanding officer. In his letter of transmission, he states that the Utah boys now serving with the 159th Field Hospital in France, read with much interest, the account of the work of the Utah soldiers as given in the February number of the *Era.--Editors.*]

The First Utah Field Hospital was mobilized and drafted into Federal service at Fort Douglas, Utah, August 5, 1917. The organization had seen service on the Mexican Border, under the command of Major John F. Sharp, but the personnel of the company as it was organized for service in the Great War consisted mainly of Utah boys, who had just enlisted.

On September 13, 1917, the First Utah Field Hospital comprising five officers and seventy-five enlisted men left Salt Lake City for Camp Kearny, California, under the command of Captain Geo. F. Roberts and Major John F. Sharp, the former commander having preceded the company by several days to act in the capacity of Director of Field Hospitals. At Camp Kearny the organization became a part of the 15th Sanitary Train, and was officially designated by the War Department as Field Hospital 159, which number they have maintained throughout the war.

The fall, winter and summer of 1917 and 1918, were spent in intensive training at Camp Kearny, most of the men and some of the officers assisting in the 40th Division Base Hospital. Of the four Field Hospitals in the 40th Division, the Utah organization made the best record in setting up hospitals under field conditions, in athletics and in general efficiency.

On July 31, 1918, the organization left Camp Kearny for Montreal, from which port it sailed August 13, 1918. After a voyage of eighteen days in a British Transport, during which many of the men suffered with influenza, it landed at Liverpool, England. Stepping from the boat to the train, the journey was continued to Southampton, and after but a few hours rest another transport was boarded, making the cross-channel trip in the darkness of the night, landing at La Havre, France, the second day of September. From La Havre the company traveled to the headquarters of the 40th Division, in central France, where the men tasted their first trouble of war by being required to sleep on the ground in the drenching rain, without protection, after days and days of weary travel and meagre meals. A long march, with wet clothes and hungry stomachs, took the organization to an old mediaeval chateau where welcomed rest was found in the horse barns of a former well-to-do Frenchmen.

For a month and a half the men worked with other sanitary troops, fitting up the chateau for a camp hospital to care for the sick men of the district. The epidemic of Spanish influenza was at that time unchecked, and many cases were treated.

Just after the hospial had started operation, the organization was ordered to the Alsace Lorraine battle front, where a great concentration of troops was then being effected for a drive on Metz, Germany's greatest fortified stronghold on the French border, the capture of which would have been the crowning achievement of America's 1918 campaign. For ten days a camp was established in a position where Uncle Sam's big guns were placed to start a new offensive against the enemy. The signing of the armistice stopped the carrying into effect of orders which, on the following day, would have taken the 159th Field Hospital well beyond the then established American lines. A short time after the cessation of hostilities the Utah men were ordered on the trail of the retreating German army, beyond the zone which had witnessed four years of battle, into former enemy territory. In connection with other medical troops, a hospital was established to care for the prisoners of war returning from Germany. The physical condition of many was indeed pathetic to behold, and valuable assistance was rendered in nursing the sick and in feeding and helping others to reach the Allied lines, further back in France. With the advance of the Armies of Occupation, the organization opened a separate hospital in a large building formerly used by the Germans for that purpose. Here its personnel is still working day and night, caring for the sick and wounded. Many casualties have occurred to the forces salvaging the battlefields, destroying the mines, time bombs, gas shells and ammunition dumps left by the Germans. During the winter months Spanish influenza and pneumonia were prevalent in the army, and the Utah boys watched at the bedside of dying comrades in arms, administering to every need and comfort of those who are far from home.

The 159th Field Hospital has received very high praise and commendation for efficient work and soldierly conduct from Train, Corps, and Army commanders and surgeons. The organization has been pronounced the most efficient in the train of which it is a part, and commanding officers have paid high tribute to the excellent character of the personnel. Of the original seventy-five enlisted men and five officers who left Salt Lake City, but forty-six enlisted men and one of the officers are still with the company, the others having been discharged because of sickness or transferred to other organizations.

Advice to Brothers

By Gus Dyer

[This soldier of Battery D, 17th Field Artillery, American Expeditionary Forces, writes from Bendorf, Germany, December 25, 1918, to his brothers, Ralph, Alvin and Mont, this message of good advice. The *Era* has been permitted to copy the letter, through the courtesy of A. R. Dyer, 142, No. 7th West St., Salt Lake City.—*Editors.*]

My Dear Brothers: I wish I could express to you boys how deeply I was moved when I heard of the death of our beloved President Joseph F. Smith. Ever since I was a boy I have looked to him for advice and have loved to hear him speak and to read his teachings. He has been a most useful and beneficent man, always doing good and trying to help others all the days of his life. From the time he crossed the plains, driving the ox teams that pulled his widowed mother, until the hour of his death, he always met up with sacrifice and service. These are two of the greatest principles that any boy, girl, man or woman can develop. Learn to do without things you would like, learn to give up to others things which you want, learn to give in to other people. Say your prayers every night and morning, and you will learn how to sacrifice. Did you ever give up any thing you would like, to make mother or father, brother or sister, or friend happy? Remember the scout law "do a kind act each day." By doing things for others is the way we really become happy. When you begin to sacrifice then you commence to serve. Service unto others is a sure means of happiness. In doing good things for others each day, never tell any body what you have done. Just foregt it, and do another good thing the next day, and then forget you did it. Each morning you wake up sing the song, "Make the world brighter today." President Smith became a great man because he learned in his boyhood to help his mother, loved ones, friends, and all whom he could. President Wilson, the great American president and leader, now in France, is a good man and a leader because his purpose is to help others. The most important command from our Savior requires us to forget ourselves and first, "Serve the Lord with all thy strength," and second, "Love thy neighbor;" which means do good to all men. Let me, your brother, because of my love for you and your welfare, encourage you to look to the teachings of the leaders of our Church, both those living and dead. There is no safer guide for your happiness. May the Lord ever grant unto you peace, and happiness and joy in life; strength in every sinew, power in the priesthood and a rich knowledge of truth, for "The truth shall make you free," all of this I promise you, and which you will understand if you keep the Word of Wisdom.

Learn to love your home and be happy in dear Salt Lake City. My sincere advice is to avoid too much amusement such as picture shows, and places of idle pleasure. You will never regret delving into books and building up in yourselves strong manhood. Be sincere, righteous, and honest. Make all your amusements good and clean, but let most of them be in your home. Boys, if you had seen what I have seen, and could feel as I feel, your home and your opportunities would be attended to with vigor and alacrity. Go to father in everything that you do, and go to him now with this letter, and talk to him and have him explain to you what the good things are in life for you. The things which will make you happy. The cause of the War is that men become dissatisfied, not knowing how to be happy. Learn while you are young to do things to make you happy. Learn to sacrifice—learn to help others—learn to obey.

My Christmas wishes to you are that you will do the thing which you know to be right each day of your life. Your future then will always be a happy one. May our heavenly Father bless you, and may mother and father become more proud of you each day of their lives.

Nothing From Nothing

Creation a Process of Organization

By Elder James. E. Talmage, of the Council of the Twelve

"In the beginning God created the heaven and the earth."
These are the opening words of the Holy Bible as we have it. The verse is at once the embodiment of simplicity and profundity. It is a masterpiece of literary summation.

Acknowledging our human limitations of comprehension, let us eliminate "the heaven" of infinite extent, and restrict our attention to the certified fact that *God created the earth.*

Many a reader has queried, though few have ventured to voice the question in definite terms: *Of what did God create the earth?*

For long ages an insufficient and unsatisfactory answer has been current—that creation means making something from nothing, and the quoted Scripture has been taken to mean that the earth, comprising land, water, air and all that in them is, were formed out of nothing. Though in acknowledged conflict with the fundamental facts demonstrated by science as to the constitution of matter, this concept of creation yet sways the thoughts of men, and is perpetuated in some modern dictionaries.

What is nothing? Lexicographers answer that "nothing" is a state of non-existence.

Granting that the finite mind is wholly unable to picture or apprehend a universal state of non-existence, we may reasonably ask, if such a state ever was, what could ever have come out of it?

Is it not a self-evident truth that from nothing nothing can come? Had there ever been a state of nothingness, that state must perforce have been of endless duration.

I know that I am, and the fact of my existence is conclusive, absolute, and incontrovertible proof that never was there a state of nothingness. The material of my body, the substance of the pen and paper with which I write, the elements of the flowers and trees I see from my window—the matter of which all material things are composed, is eternal. It has always existed and always will exist.

True, I have not always existed in my present embodied condition; nor has the desk that just now facilitates my writing always existed as a desk. Furthermore, the elements of my body have not always been combined in their present association as flesh, blood, and bone, nor the elements of my desk as wood.

Unseen processes of absorption and assimilation drew in, with discriminating selection, certain gases of the air, certain chemical compounds from the soil, and so nurtured the tree, from a sprouting seed to the fully matured trunk from which the artizan shaped, or created if you will, my desk.

Reason asserts that God did not create the earth out of nothing. There is no sacrilege in saying that He could not have done so.

With skill and power infinitely exceeding all that man has acquired, God took of eternally existent matter and formed therefrom the earth with all its material accessories and belongings. Unbounded and illimitable space is full of material, out of which the Divine Chemist can compound as He wills, and He may cause worlds to come into existence as worlds, created out of the once formless and void, but nevertheless pre-existent, matter.

As matter in the ultimate sense cannot be created or made, it necessarily follows that matter cannot be destroyed. This desk may be burned and so disappear, both as the fashioned furniture and as the combination of elements that constitute the wood; but the indestructible elements are only released and returned to the current of circulation.

The word of latter-day revelation, given by the Lord through His prophet Joseph Smith, is explicit in demonstrating that what we call the creation of the world was a process of organization of preexistent elements. Thus we read that in the beginning—that is to say before the earth was formed—in the conclave of unembodied spirits, God spake, saying: *"We will go down, for there is space there, and we will take of these materials, and we will make an earth whereon these may dwell."* (Pearl of Great Price, p. 66).

In distinguishing between intelligent spirits, and the material bodies in which for the period of earth-life they live, the Lord hath said: *"For man is spirit. The elements are eternal, and spirit and element, inseparably connected, receiveth a fulness of joy. The elements are the tabernacle of God; yea, man is the tabernacle of God, even temples; and whatsoever temple is defiled, God shall destroy that temple."* (Doctrine and Covenants 93:33, 35).

Basis of True Religion

The basis of true religion is a knowledge of God. "This is life eternal, that they might know thee the only true God, and Jesus Christ, whom thou hast sent."

In order that we may have a basis for true religion, we must believe that God is and that he is a rewarder of them that diligently seek him. We must learn his personality, character and will.

Naturally, then, the question arises, how shall we come to a knowledge of God?

In our early catechism for children by that veteran teacher, Elder John Jaques, we were given an answer to this question: there are three ways in which mankind may learn that there is a God. First, by tradition, second by reason, and third by revelation. Then he goes on to tell us how: parents tell their children, who in turn tell their children, and so on the knowledge is handed down for ages, and men learn by tradition that there is a God.

Mankind learn by reason that there is a God by looking around them and beholding his works in nature. They watch the seasons come and go in regular order. They see the sun shine by day, the moon and stars by night, and behold the order of the heavens, with all its marvelous changes. They see the rains descend, the fruits and verdure of the earth appear in their seasons, and as all these things cannot be stopped, nor the times when they appear be altered by men, the conclusion is that there must be a Being with superior intelligence who governs and directs all things. In this way, one learns by reason that there is a God.

By revelation one learns by God himself appearing to men, or sending angels to them, who have greater power and knowledge and glory than man; or He speaks to them by his own voice from the heavens, or gives them dreams and visions, and in this way, men learn by revelation, that there is a God.

The first two methods of learning are indistinct and unsatisfactory, and only by revelation can a definite and satisfactory knowledge be obtained. One need not quote the examples of this truth found in many passages of the holy scriptures. In modern times, the Father has appeared with his

Son Jesus Christ, to the Prophet Joseph Smith, spoken to him, given him instructions, and made themselves known, revealing to mankind anew that they exist and are in the likeness of man. The word of scripture is indeed proved true, that God created man in his own image, in the image of God created he him, male and female created he them.

The foundation of the religion of the Latter-day Saints is thus laid first and foremost upon a knowledge of a personal God, received through revelation to the Prophet Joseph Smith, and confirmed by personal testimony to every truly repentant believer, by the Holy Ghost.

Every person is entitled to this same revelation who seeks for it in the way that the Prophet Joseph Smith sought: "If any of you lack wisdom, let him ask of God, who giveth to all men liberally and upbraideth not, and it shall be given him." Believing this, Joseph went to the Lord in the only way that a man may approach him; namely, through prayer. The wisdom that he desired was granted unto him, as it will be to all who approach Father in like manner, nothing doubting.

The knowledge of God, then, through personal contact, is the basis of all true religion—the safe and only road to salvation. The first and great commandment is: "Thou shalt love the Lord thy God with all thy might, mind and strength," and the second, as Christ explained, is like unto it: "Thou shalt love thy neighbor as thyself." The order in which these commandments are placed, is the true order: first, love the Lord thy God; second, love thy neighbor as thyself. Upon these two commandments, according to the Savior, hang all the law and the prophets. It is impossible to love God with all one's heart, without loving one's neighbor. While the reverse, loving one's neighbor, may not always lead to a true love of God. A true conception of God, his character and will, influences men to human duty as defined in true morality and love of mankind. Separated from the love of God, morality, and social efficiency, in themselves, never can become a basis of true religion. The order is service to God first, then unselfish service to man must and will follow. We do not think we are far from the truth when we say that without first rendering unselfish service to God, and obedience to his commandments, the plan which Jesus Christ established in the earth for the salvation of men, true and unselfish service to mankind will never come. There will be no peace in the earth that will be permanent until mankind shall recognize the gospel of Jesus Christ, first learn to know the true and living God, and Jesus Christ whom he has sent. But with this knowledge will come peace and eternal life to those who walk in the pathway.

True religion, founded in the character and will of God, always influences to noble action and to love of neighbor, springing from the love of God. A true knowledge of Him does not permit a man to let his feelings and emotions end in themselves, but it stimulates him to acts of mercy, kindness, and love. Thus, one must first seek for the knowledge of God, his will and his righteousness, and all other things will be added unto him, until religion shall become a working fact, a standard philosophy, an influence that moves to human duty, founded in the character and will of God, to whom obedience, service and honor are due. Having rendered such service, obedience, honor and recognition to Him, men cannot fail to serve their neighbors and humanity, thus fulfiling the second great commandment: "Thou shalt love thy neighbor as thyself."

The religion of the Latter-day Saints teaches duty to God first, and obedience to his will, and having fulfiled those requirements, the believer is ready and prepared to fulfil his duty to man, thus complying with both requirements of the law expressed by the Savior: "Thou shalt love the Lord thy God with all thy might, mind and strength, and thy neighbor as thyself."

The religion of the Latter-day Saints is spiritual, intellectual, and practical. Its emotions do not end in emotions, but in noble action. Its philosophy is rational, is based on a true knowledge of God, and leads to a practical fulfilment of his holy will. Its doctrines are clearcut interpretations of the message delivered by the Redeemer of mankind to the world. They are based upon a proper conception of God, faith in his revealed will and action in conformity to that will. The spiritual, the temporal, the emotional, the practical in the faith of the Latter-day Saints are so combined that the believers are enabled to be as they are, and should be, true lovers of God, the Eternal Father, and of his Son Jesus Christ, and the plan of salvation which they have revealed for the exaltation of man, as well as lovers of mankind and practical helpers in the uplift of humanity.

Commendable Activity

Scarcely a returning soldier from overseas, but has the warmest sympathy and commendation in his heart for the Salvation Army. These people were with the boys at the front and in the trenches, looking after their needs, providing them with little necessaries and comforts to gladden their hearts, relieving their wants, pains and sorrows, to an extent that no orther organization did. The service was done, too, without price or selfish motives.

As an example, one little incident may be cited. When

a ship arrived in New York recently, carrying a number of our Utah boys on their return from overseas, they were met on shipboard before landing, as many other soldiers had been met, by Salvation Army representatives, with prepared telegrams which they asked the boys to sign. These telegrams notified the home folks of their loved ones' safe return to New York. Many were signed by the boys, and a number were received in various parts of the State of Utah, being sent free directly to the folks at home by the Salvation Army representatives. It was a simple message: "Arrived safely in New York, all well," or words to that effect, but only the folks at home could appreciate the service or know the gladness of the message.

On April 24, the telegram was followed by a little letter sent to the father or mother at home and which read as follows:

"*Dear Sir:* You will have received our telegram conveying the glad news of the safe arrival from overseas of your relative. [Son or friend, as the case might be].

"I send you this letter to say how much we rejoice with you in the happiness which this homecoming will bring, and to assure you of our prayers that our heavenly Father, who has been so good in bringing back the one you love, will continue to bless you and him. I want to assure you that you will find us ever ready to help you in any way possible.

"Wishing you every blessing, sincerely yours,
"*Evangeline Booth,* Commander."

This may seem a simple and a little thing to do, but all persons who received such a message will forever after have a loving thought in their hearts for the organization and its workers who took the time and trouble without reward or remuneration, to perform this little service, which means so much to those unto whom it was rendered. It is an indication of the attention they paid to the boys in the camps and at the front, amenities which have made the returned soldier so full of praise for the lassies of the Salvation Army!

Messages from the Missions

Good Work of the Bureau of Information

Leon M. Strong, secretary of the Northern States mission, Chicago, Illinois, under date of April 11, says that the office has a list of earnest investigators to whom they send the *Era* occasionally, and they have received letters of appreciation for the favor. The *Era* finds a hearty welcome with the missionaries and their friends. He continues: "The excellent missionary work done by the Bureau of Information, and the directors of the organ recitals in the tabernacle, Salt Lake City, is effective in making lasting friends from various parts of the country, who are happy to tell missionaries, on meeting them, of the pleasant experiences on the Temple grounds. Needless to say, the missionaries always find a true friend in such people. We wish you continued success for your splendid magazine." The following

are the missionaries laboring in Chicago, front row, left to right: George W. Fowler, mission clerk; D. Rees Jensen, Mrs. Mary Smith Ellsworth; President German E. Ellsworth; Paul S. Hansen, president Chicago conference; Franklin S. Davis, mission stenographer; Clarence E. Schank, mission bookkeeper. Second row: Levi Swensen, Lexia M. Clark, Carl F. Reimann, Sam H. Williams, Allie L. Carlston, Marjory Howard, Douglas O. Woodruff, Richard P. Condie. Third row: Matilda Nuttall, O. D. Van Orden, N. Cassie Stevens, Anders Anderson, Florence Telford, Leon M. Strong, mission secretary; Clara Devy.

An Occasional Sounding for Bed Rock

"We thank Thee O God for a Prophet," has been sung by and recorded on the Columbia Graphophone for sometime. Recently the proprietor of a New York Undertaking Parlor, Henn Brothers, wrote to the Eastern States Mission of the Church, asking them to send the words and music of this beautiful song for use in their parlors. The Eastern States Mission referred the matter to the Northern States Mission at Chicago, Illinois, and a copy of the *Songs of Zion* was sent to the firm, which later expressed the desire to have the L. D. S. male or mixed quartet come and sing some of the hymns contained in the *Songs of Zion* at the funerals held in their parlors. Leon M. Strong, Secretary of the Northern States mission writes: "This incident together with many letters coming into the office asking for Books of Mormon and Doctrine and Covenants, makes us feel encouraged in the thought that 'Mormonism' has stood the test, and the pendulum has started to swing back in our direction. Through the great wave of indifference in general, and prejudice towards the Latterday Saints in particular, there comes an occasional sounding for bedrock on the part of those at sea spiritually."

Sixty Lady Missionaries in the Field.

Elder Joseph S. Nelson, Bradford, England, writes under date of April 15: "The enclosed photo includes most of the elders present at the Leeds General conference, held at Westgate Hall, Bradford, March 30. After being alone in the conference for some little while, it was truly a treat to have so many elders together here. Chaplain Calvin Smith, now on leave to take a three months' course at the Leed's University, stands in the center, the other three who are standing are English boys who are on missions, paying their own expenses, just as do the elders from Zion: They are left to right Ira William Mount, Liverpool; E. Henry Clark, Birmingham, president; Reginald H. Sanders, Leeds. Those sitting are left to right: Ether L. Marley, Liverpool; Joseph S. Nelson, Leeds, retiring president; Arnold G. Holland, Leeds, incoming president; Orial L. Anderson, Norwich,

retiring president. Mission President George F. Richards is now releasing many of the few remaining American missionaries to return home. Local brethren are taking their places, in many instances, as conference presidents. Already four traveling elders have been called out of this conference alone, within two months. We have sixty local lady missionaries, each reporting work done for each month this year. Fifteen people were baptized in February, and we are already prepared for another baptism company. It is a glorious work."

Program

FOURTEEN—SUMMER WORK

Tuesday Evening, July 8, 1919.

General Subject: *Peace Conference Program.*
Topic: *"Re-drawing the World's Map."*

M. I. A. Annual Conference

Salt Lake City, June 6, 7, 8, 1919

PROGRAM—FRIDAY, JUNE 6

Joint M. I. A. Officers' Meeting, Assembly Hall, 10 a. m.

1. Opening Hymn, "Behold a Royal Army"........ ....Congregation
2. Prayer
3. Chorus........................."A C ppella" Club—Mrs. Esther Stephens, Director
4. The M. I. A. Slogan: "We Stand for Spiritual Growth through Attendance at Sacrament Meetings.'
    "And that thou mayest more fully keep thyself unspotted from the world, thou shalt go to the house of prayer and offer up thy sacraments upon my holy day." (Doc. and Cov. Sec. 59:9.)
5. Greetings .... Presiding Officers
6. Advanced Senior Class Work...............................Dr. George H. Brimhall
7. Chorus .... "A Cappella" Club
8. Teacher Training Classes—(a) Organization and plan; (b) Lesson and application; (c) The spirit of teaching....................Elder David O. McKay Discussion.
9. Closing Hymn, "Onward Christian Soldiers"...........................Congregation
10. Benediction.

Separate Y. M. M. I. A. Officers' Meeting, Bishop's Building, 2 p. m.

1. Opening exercise.
2. Roll call and reports.
3. M. I. A. Slogan: "We Stand for Spiritual Growth through Attendance at Sacrament Meetings."
    "Thou shalt love the Lord thy God with all thy heart, with all thy might, mind, and strength; and in the name of Jesus Christ thou shalt serve him." (Doc. and Cov. 59:5.)
4. Junior Deaprtment—"Our Biggest Problem—Suggestions for Its Solution"—(a) Organization, George J. Cannon; (b) Leadership, B. F. Grant; (c) Activities, John H. Taylor; (d) Summary, B. S. Hinckley.
5. Closing exercises.

Separate Y. L. M. I. A. Officers' Meeting, Assembly Hall, 2 p. m.

1. Opening hymn, "Earth With Her Ten Thousand Flowers'....Congregation
2. Prayer.
3. Chorus.............Wilford Ward Ladies' Chorus—Mrs. Ida White, Director
4. Roll and report.
5. "We Stand for Spiritual Growth through Attendance at Sacrament Meetings."
    "And he said unto them, he that eateth this bread, eateth of my body to his soul, and he that drinketh of this wine, drinketh of my blood to his soul, and his soul shall never hunger nor thirst, but shall be filled." (III Nephi 20:8.)

6. Opening Remarks.....................................President Martha H. Tingey
7. Solo ....Florence Summerhays
8. Junior Work ....Ann M. Cannon
9. Senior Work ....Lucy Grant Cannon
10. Social Service.
11. Chorus...Wilford Ward Ladies' Chorus
12. Benediction.

Joint Y. M. and Y. L. M. I. A. Reception and Social to Visiting Stake Officers

Roof Garden, Joseph F. Smith Memorial Building, Latter-day Saints
University, 8 p. m.

SATURDAY, JUNE 7

Joint M. I. A. Officers' Meeting, Assembly Hall, 10 a. m.

1. Opening Hymn, "We Are All Enlisted"..................................Congregation
2. Prayer.
3. String trio........Misses Lucille Schettler, Margaret and Katherine Stewart
4. "We Stand for Spiritual Growth through Attendance at Sacrament Meetings."
   "And there was one day in every week that was set apart that they should gather themselves together to teach the people, and to worship the Lord their God, and also as often as it was in their power, to assemble themselves together." (Mosiah 18:25.)
5. Announcement of M. I. A. Activities.............................Mary E. Connelly
6. M. I. A. Service..LeRoi C. Snow
7. Solo..Mrs. Nellie Thomas
8. Summer Work—(a) Why this work? (b) The program; (c) Leadership, Mrs. Martha G. Smith; (d) Publicity and problems and solution, Roscoe W. Eardley.
9. Closing hymn, "We are Watchers, Earnest Watchers".........Congregation
10. Prayer.

Separate Y. M. M. I. A. Officers' Meeting, Bishop's Building, 2 p. m.

1. Opening Exercises.
2. Roll and miscellaneous reports.
3. M. I. A. Slogan: "We Stand for Spiritual Growth through Attendance at Sacrament Meetings."
   "Jesus took bread and blessed it, and gave it to the disciples and said, Take, eat; this is my body. And he took the cup and gave thanks, and gave it to them, saying, Drink ye all of it, for this is my blood of the New Testament, which is shed for many for the remission of sins." (Matt. 26:28.)
4. Responsibility of the Senior Department.................Osborne J. P. Widtsoe
5. Each Lesson Faith Promoting..............................Henry C. Lund
6. The Test of Efficiency...................................Nephi Anderson
7. Finance .... Claude Richards
8. Publications .... Preston Nibley
9. Closing Exercises.

Separate Y. L. M. I. A. Officers' Meeting, Assembly Hall, 2 p. m.

1. Opening Hymn, "Count Your Blessings"..............................Congregation
2. Prayer.
3. Solo...Edith Grant Young
4. "We Stand for Spiritual Growth through Attendance at Sacrament Meetings."
   "And this shall ye always observe to do, even as I have done, even as I have broken bread, and blessed it, and gave it unto you.

* * * And I give unto you a commandment that ye shall do these things. And if ye shall always do these things, blessed are ye, for ye are built upon my rock." (III Nephi 18:6, 12.)

5. Address..President Heber J. Grant
6. Closing Hymn, "High on the Mountain Top"....................Congregation

Executive Session, 3 p. m.

Final Contests in Public Speaking, Assembly Hall, 7:30 p. m.

SUNDAY, JUNE 8

Officers' Testimony Meeting, Assembly Hall, 8:30 a. m.

1. Opening Hymn, "Glory to God on High"....................Congregation
2. Prayer.
3. Hymn, "Oh, Say What is Truth"....................Congregation
4. Closing Hymn, "Do What is Right"....................Congregation

Joint Officers' Meeting, Tabernacle, 10 a. m.

1. Opening Hymn, "Come, Let Us Anew"....................Congregation
2. Prayer.
3. Male Chorus....................S. D. Winter, Director
4. "We Stand for Spiritual Growth through Attendance at Sacrament Meetings."

"But remember that on this the Lord's day, thou shalt offer thine oblations and thy sacraments unto the Most High. * * * And on this day thou shalt do none other thing only let thy food be prepared with singleness of heart that thy fasting may be perfect, or in other words, that thy joy may be full." (Doc. and Cov. 59:12,13.)

5. Selection .... Male Chorus
6. "A Campaign for 100,000 Membership"—(a) Purpose and plan of the campaign, Assistant Superintendent Richard R. Lyman; (b) The Value of the M. I. A. in My Stake, President E. J. Wood, Alberta Stake; (c) What the M. I. A. has done for me (two ten-minute talks), Lorenzo Young, Mollie Higginson.
7. Ladies' Chorus....................Margaret Summerhays, Conductor
6. (d) Advertising the M. I. A., Claude Richards; (e) Holding the 100,000, Ernest P. Horsley.
8. Closing Hymn, "Guide Us, O Thou Great Jehovah"............Congregation
9. Benediction.

Public Meeting in the Tabernacle, 2 p. m.

"We Stand for Spiritual Growth through Attendance at Sacrament Meetings."
"And the Church did meet together oft, to fast and to pray, and to speak with one another concerning the welfare of their souls; And they did meet together oft to partake of bread and wine, in remembrance of the Lord Jesus." (Moroni 6:5, 6.)
This meeting will be under the direction of the General Church Authorities. Music for this session will be furnished by the Tabernacle Choir—Prof. A. C. Lund, Director; Prof. J. J. McClellan at the Organ ·

Public Meeting in the Tabernacle, 7:30 p. m.

Music for this session will be furnished by the Tabernacle Choir—Prof. A. C. Lund, Director; Prof. J. J. McClellan at the Organ.
1. Opening Exercises.
2. "We Stand for Spiritual Growth through Attendance at Sacrament Meetings."
"And this shall ye do in remembrance of my body, which I have shewn unto you. And it shall be a testimony unto the Father,

that ye do always remember me. And if ye do always remember me, ye shall have my Spirit to be with you. * * *

"And when the disciples had done this Jesus said unto them, Blessed are ye for this thing which ye have done, for this is fulfilling my commandments, and this doth witness unto the Father that ye are willing to do that which I have commanded you." (III Nephi 18:7, 10.)

3. The M. I. A. Slogan—(a) Communion with Saints; (b) "Faith cometh by hearing," Counselor Ruth May Fox; (c) The Sacramental covenant and blessing—Elder Melvin J. Ballard.

4. Closing Exercises.

Commendable Scout Activity

A report of the scout scribe of Troop 44, M. I. A., Emerson ward, Granite stake, is a fine sample of what many like troops of boy scouts of Salt Lake City are accomplishing. The report covers the work between the period March 19, 1918, to March 18, 1919.

The disbursements are as follows:

Printing of programs and other expenses of scout play of March 22, 1918	$ 78.35
Ward donations	15.00
Mutual Improvement Association	15.00
Janitor service	6.00
Scout party, ice cream, etc.	3.00
Registration fee for the troop	18.25
Troop flags and other supplies	1.20
Flowers of sympathy	2.00
Swimming lessons	5.50
Expenses for auto service and supplies on hikes	17.11
Liberty Bond	51.00
Total	$212.41

Making a balance of $21.31 in the treasury.

In addition to being the only scout troop to purchase a Liberty Bond out of troop funds, we have taken active part in the following campaigns: Red Cross service for old clothes, magazines, books and distributing advertising literature, distributing Liberty Loan bills on the second drive at 9 p. m., distributing Extras on two occasions at 6 a. m., stake and church tabernacle patrol duty on several occasions.

We have gathered fast offerings during the Influenza epidemic and are scouting such service up to date. In one of the best months of such service we collected over $50 for which our bishop has given us due credit. We have a number of boys who sold bonds in every issue. Three boys obtained their ace medals in Thrift Stamp sales. We have ten boys who went over the top in the last Liberty Loan drive, and, through the determination and good salesmanship of the boys, we ranked fourth among the troops in the entire city for total sales. We expect to do big things in the Victory Drive.

Besides the above mentioned, we have aided a number of widows in the ward to spade and prepare war gardens. You will see that there has been a number of things accomplished by the troop that most of the people are not aware of, and we solicit your support to make this a better and bigger troop.

Every scout in our troop, of which we are all proud to be members, is trying to live up to the scout promise and law.

Edward Taggart, *Scout Scribe.*
Wm. A. Dunn, *Scoutmaster.*

PASSING EVENTS

Former Kaiser Wilhelm, according to a provision in the Peace Treaty, will be brought before a court of five judges composed of representatives of the United States, Great Britain, France, Italy, and Japan, and tried for his crimes.

Honorable Anthony W. Ivins, was chosen president of the Board of Trustees of the Agriculture College of Utah, and John Dern of Salt Lake City, vice-president, at the regular annual re-organization meeting of the Board, held at the college on Saturday, April 26. President Ivins succeeds Lorenzo N. Stohl, who has been a board member for fourteen years, and who has acted as president of the board for twelve years. Mr. Stohl having resigned, he was tendered a vote of thanks for his long and efficient services as chief executive.

President Carranza of Mexico, is making himself as dis greeable as possible to the Allied nations. Mexico has declined to recognize the clause in the Armistice of November 11, 1918, which pledged Germany not to dispose of any of its foreign security without Allied consent, on the ground that Mexican law was contravened thereby. Mexico also publicly protested against the Monroe Doctrine, as an attack on the sovereignty of Mexico. The withdrawal of its representatives at Paris and Rome followed. France and Italy, have both declined to recognize the Carranza government.

Dr. Heber John Richards, one of Utah's medical pioneers, died at his home in Provo, on Monday, May 12, 1919. He was born in Manchester, England, October 11, 1840; coming to Utah with his parents when a young man. He received his early education in the Deseret University, and later graduated, with the degree of Doctor of Medicine, from the Bellvue Medical college, New York, and was considered for many years, Utah's foremost physician, being associated in Salt Lake City, with the late Doctor W. F. Anderson. In 1892, he went to Provo, where he practiced medicine for many years.

A special session of Congress was called by proclamation of President Wilson, by cable from France, May 7, to convene at 12 noon, May 19, 1917, at Washington. The sixty-sixth, or "reconstruction" congress was organized by electing Representative Gillett of Massachusetts, speaker of the House; and Senator Cummings of Iowa, president pro tem. of the Senate, both Republicans, which party now assumes control for the first time since 1911, of the National Legislature. A short message from President Wilson was read, May 20. The League of Nations, the Peace Treaty and the failed appropriation bills will receive attention first.

The cable systems between the United States and Europe, taken over by the Government sometime ago, reverted to their private owners at midnight, May 2. Postmaster-General Burleson, recommended on April 28, that the telegraph and telephone lines also be returned to the control of the companies owning them, at the earliest possible date. The increase of telegraph and telephone rates ordered by the Government, were enjoined in the state of Illinois, by Judge Landis, of the United States Court, who granted an injunction forbidding the postmaster-general from enforcing the increased telegraph rates within that state. The opinion held that the Federal power to fix rates, did not extend to rates between points entirely within a single state.

Dynamite bombs, carefully made, and mailed as parcel-post packages, were discovered in the New York postoffice on April 30. They were all dressed to well known men throughout the United States, including Justice Holmes of the Supreme Court, Postmaster-General Burleson, Secretary of Labor Wilson, Mayor Hanson of Seattle and others. Two of the bombs arrived at postoffices in Utah, designed for Senator William H. King, and Aquilla Nebeker. One bomb delivered at the home of Former Senator Hardwick, of Georgia, exploded and blew off the hands of a negro servant The plot was discovered in time to prevent further danger or injury by these packages which were sent out to destroy life by anarchist agitators who planned the murder of every federal official who had been concerned in the execution of the espionage law and the deportation of anarchist aliens. The bombs were sent from New York, April 30.

Heber C. Smith, formerly state Dairy and Food commissioner and later of the Juvenile Court, Salt Lake City, son of President Joseph F. Smith, has been chosen to take charge of the Joseph Smith Memorial Farm, at South Royalton, Vermont. Mrs. Frank M. Brown and son Kenneth who, since the death by influenza of Elder Brown, on New Years' day, 1919, have had charge of the farm, have been honorably released. Mr. and Mrs. Brown went to South Royalton nine years ago, when the tract now occupied by the memorial was only a barren, rocky stretch. Under their care it has been transformed into a model farm, with up-to-date barns, dairy, and sheep herds. Four hundred acres, or more of land belong to the farm upon which the Prophet Joseph Smith was born, and upon which the memorial was built some fifteen years ago. From three to four thousand tourists have been entertained upon the grounds every summer. Frequently 75 to 100 auto parties visit the home every Sunday.

The Bolshiviki in Russia, are said to be disintegrating; discouraged by the steady hostility of the peasantry and the difficulty of getting supplies, they have failed on every side. Practically surrounded by armies, Soviet, Russia is hemmed in, and there is every reason to believe at this writing, that Alexander Vassilievitch Kolchak, the Russian admiral and the most prominent leader of the forces opposing the Bolshivik regime will evolve order out of the sanguinary chaos and devastation that have reigned in the once mighty empire of the Czars for the last two years. At this writing there is every prospect that he will become the ruler of Russia as he is now the dictator of Omsk, Siberia. The Bolshiviki have made a bitter struggle against all the economic and social laws which have hitherto governed mankind. Bolshivism, Communism, Spartacism, everywhere is waning perceptibly. Reports are insistent, that the military forces of the Lenine regime are becoming demoralized, and that some divisions have mutined.

Report of Changes in Ward and Stake Officers, April, 1919. New Wards and Bishops.—Idaho Falls, 2nd ward, Bingham stake, David Smith, bishop, address Idaho Falls, Idaho.

Ogden 14th ward, Weber stake, Clarence Morris, bishop.

New Bishops.—Fairview ward, Oneida stake, William Harvey Wiser succeeded Edwin Bodily, address same. Preston 4th ward, Oneida stake, John W. Condie succeeded Wm. A. Skidmore, address same. Glencoe ward, Oneida stake, Parley P. Carver succeeded Carl E. Peterson, address same. Helper branch, Carbon stake, Claude Brown, P. E. Tyhee ward, Pocatello stake, Omni Porter succeeded Abinadi Porter, address same. Second ward, Liberty stake, Henry B. Elder succeeded Heber C. Iverson, address 843 So. 5th East, City. Eighth ward, Liberty stake, John Fetzer succeeded Oscar F. Hunter, address 579 Hamilton Court, City. Thirty-third ward Liberty stake, Charles E. Forsberg succeeded Edwin S. Sheets, address 1327 East 4th South, City.

Fletcher B. Hammond, Moab, for eight years a representative in the state legislature of Utah from Grand county, and one of the best known business men in the Southern part of our state, died in a local hospital, Salt Lake City, May 3, 1919, from injuries suffered on April 19, when his clothing was caught in the machinery of a power plant at his home. Fletcher B. Hammond, was born in the Sandwich Islands, March 31, 1855, his parents, Bishop Francis A. Hammond and wife Jane Dillworth Hammond, being there on a mission for the Church. His early life was spent in Ogden and Huntsville, in which latter place her married Calista O. Bronson, who died after his removal to Moab. Mr. Hammond became interested in sheep and cattle, and later engaged in the mercantile business as well. When he had come to man's estate he went on a mission to Britian, and six sons have also served the Church in the mission field. He is survived by his widow, Ida Weston Hammond, and eight children, among them Bishop Clyde Hammond, Moab, Bishop Dillworth Hammond, Lasalle, Utah. The body was taken to Moab for funeral services and interment.

Patriarch Thomas Atkin died in Tooele, April 18, 1919, at the residence of his son Willard G. Atkin. He was born July 7, 1833, in South Lincolnshire, England and baptized a member of the Church on July 3, 1843. From the age of 14 up to the time his parents emigrated, in 1848, he aided the elders in the distributing of tracts and in preaching the gospel. Their home was long the head-quarters of the elders on missions at that time. They crossed the ocean in 1848, five of the twelve apostles of the Church, being in the company, Orson Spencer being in charge. They arrived in Salt Lake City, September 25, 1848, where they remained for three years, and then removed to Tooele, being among the first settlers of that town. On May 20, 1856, Thomas Atkin married Mary Ann Maughn, daughter of Bishop Peter Maughn, the first bishop and president of the Cache stake of Zion. For twenty-seven years Elder Atkin labored in the bishopric of Tooele, being set apart October 31, 1880, as bishop and having served as councilor to Bishop Norton Tuttle from 1877 until that date. He was ordained a patriarch by President Joseph F. Smith in 1905. He was a member of the Constitutional Convention and had served in a number of expeditions against the Indians. His whole life, was one of activity and service to the people.

The League of Nations revised covenant, was made public April 27. The new and most important changes are those that provide for a nation's withdrawal from the League on a two years notice; that require unanimity in the decisions of both the assembly and council of the League; that exempt matter properly subject to domestic jurisdiction from the action of the League; and that recognizes specifically the validity of the Monroe Doctrine. The seat of the administration of the League is established at Geneva. Amendments of the covenant by a majority vote are permitted. A number of the articles were re-written in order to make them more explicit. Thirty-two states are named as original members of the League, and thirteen others are invited to accede to the covenant. None of the enemy nations of the Allies, or those leagued with Germany, are at present included in either list, neither is the Republic of Mexico, which is out on its own request, being opposed to the Monroe Doctrine, believing it to be an attack on that nation's sovereignty. With the changes now made, it is thought that the Senate of the United States will ratify the covenant. Japan and some other nations, however, were opposed to the new changes made. The new covenant was adopted on April 28, by the Peace Conference in plenary sessions. It was adopted without a dissenting vote. The representative of Japan, however, made a final attempt to obtain the inclusion of the amendment forbidding any national legislation discriminating against persons of any race whatever. The first Secretary-General of the League, was named in the person of Sir James Eric Drummond, a prominent and permanent official of the British foreign office, and private secretary to A. J. Balfour.

Three American giant naval hydro-airplanes N C's-1, 3, and 4, commissioned to attempt a trans-Atlantic flight began the first leg of the journey on the first week of May, from Rockaway Beach, New York to Halifax, leaving the latter place for Trepassey, N. F., from which they were to leave for Lisbon, Portugal with a proposed stop at the Azores. The N. C.'s-1, 3, 4, left Trepassey, N. F., May 16, about 6:00 p. m., on New York time for the Azores, and four hours later they were reported 300 miles out. The planes and supplies weigh about 28,800 pounds. Commander Towers of the American aerial trans-Atlantic expedition has compared the three big seaplanes to the caravels of Columbus, adding that when Portugal is reached the NC's-1, 3 and 4 will be re-christened Nina, Santa Maria and Pinta respectively.

Commander Towers will direct the flight from NC-3, which will be named Santa Maria, in honor of the flagship of America's discoverer.

The Azores, the port of call four centuries ago for the ocean pioneer sailing westward, will be the first stop of the Americans flying eastward.

Wireless messages sent broadcast from Lisbon will announce the arrival of the Santa Maria, Nina and Pinta.

Incidentally, when the seaplanes reach the Azores they will, strictly speaking, have reached Europe, just as Columbus was considered to have reached the new world, when he landed at San Salvador, for the Azores are Portuguese possessions charted as the western islands of Europe.

Thus, notwithstanding whether Lisbon and Plymouth are reached by the American seaplanes touching the Azores, they will have the honor of being the first flying craft to cross the Atlantic.

All means are adopted for the safety of the aviators, twenty five cruisers being stationed on the Trepassey, Azores leg, with radio communication to indicate conditions of the flyers, and the true course to the next vessels. They traveled over 60 miles per hour at a height of about 5,000 feet. NC-4 arrived at the Azores first on Saturday morning, May 17. NC-1 and 3 were disabled, but were towed into port without loss of life. On the 19th, Harry G. Hawker, an Australian, left St. Johns, N. F., for England, but up to the morning of the 21st had not been heard from, and hopes of his recovery are abandoned.

The Peace Terms of the Allies were presented, under the presidency of Georges Clemenceau, the French Premier, to the German peace delegation at Versailles in a momentous session of the Peace Congress on Wednesday, May 7, 1919. Count von Brockdorff-Rantzau, the German foreign minister in the Ebert government was chairman of the German peace delegation. Germany protested that the terms of peace as offered were "unbearable" and "impracticable." The terms are contained in a treaty in French and English, of some 80,000 words in length, and were handed to the German plenipotentionies at the memorable assemblage attended by 27 nations, parties to the peace pact. It provides for the end of Hun militarism, deprives Germany of practically all her fleet, hedges her about economically, and prevents her from exploiting her resources for strangling smaller nations about her. In numerous ways Germany is made to realize that she must make good her more than four years career of destruction. The United States was represented by Presi. dent Wilson and Great Britain by Lloyd George, Italy by Premier Orlando.

The Literary Digest summarizes the pact of a "firm, just, and durable peace, as follows:

Germany cedes to France Alsace-Lorraine (5,600 square miles); to Belgium 387 square miles of Rhenish Prussia; to Poland, part of Silesia, most of Posen, and all of West Prussia (27,686 square miles).

Sarre Valley internationalized fifteen years, its coal-mines go to France.

Luxemburg freed from German customs control.

Danzig with adjacent territory internationalized, East Prussia isolated.

About a third of East Prussia to decide by plebiscite between Germany and Poland.

Schleswig to decide by a series of plebiscites between Germany and Denmark.

Germany gives up all colonies and rights outside of Europe.

Germany recognizes independence of German Austria, Poland, and the Czecho-Slovak state.

Germany razes all forts thirty-three miles east of the Rhine; abolishes conscription; reduces armies to 100,000 long-enlistment volunteers; reduces Navy to 6 battle-ships, 6 cruisers, 12 torpedo-boats, and personnel of 15,000; dismantles Helgoland, opens Kiel Canal to the world, and surrenders 14 ocean cables; is to have no submarines or war aircraft; stops import, export, and nearly all production of war-material.

Germany agrees to trial of ex-Kaiser and other offenders against humanity.

Germany accepts responsibility for all damages to Allied governments and peoples, agrees to restore invaded areas and to pay for shipping destruction ton for ton. The first indemnity payment is $5,000,000,000, further payments expected to bring total to at least $25,000,000,000, and details to be arranged by an Allied commission.

Partial Allied military occupation of Germany until reparation is made.

Germany accepts League of Nations without present membership; the League to control mandatories, internationalized territory, and plebiscites.

Germany grants free Allied transit through territories and certain Allied control of finance, business, and transportation on railroads, canals, and rivers.

Germany accepts all arrangements to be made with her former allies.

Germany annuls Russian and Roumanian treaties and recognizes independence of Russian states.

International labor organization and standards instituted.

Chicago has more telephones than all France, Kansas City has more telephones than Belgium, and Boston has more telephones than Austria-Hungary. Great Britain and Ireland together have only 200,000 more telephones than New York City, and some American office buildings and hotels have more telephones than the kingdom of Greece or Bulgaria. And America excels also in the quality of its telephone service. Suburban connections that can be made in half a minute in America take half an hour in London. And yet not very many years ago the *London Times* denounced the telephone as "the latest American humbug."—*Youth's Companion.*

"The *Improvement Era* has reached me every month since I have been here
writes a soldier from France, "and I can assure you that it has been read, not on
by me, but I have put it in the Y. M. C. A., and many others have found somethi
interesting within its covers. My experience has been very interesting to me, and
can now see how small one is on this great universe."

"The *Era* is doing much good where it is read with a desire to learn the tru
concerning our Church and the principles we uphold. There are some people to who
a person cannot talk, but who will take time to read; and never have I heard o
such, or any other person, remark that his time was not well spent by reading t
Era. Through the kindness of one of my sisters, the *Era* has been sent me, and up
returning home I expect it always to be on hand in my home.--*Corp. D. R. Brou
H. Q. Co., 129 F. A., A. E. F.*

Improvement Era, June, 1919

Two Dollars per Annum

Entered at the Post Office, Salt Lake City, Utah, as second class matt

*Acceptance for mailing at special rate of postage provided for in Section 1103, Act
October 3, 1917, authorized on July 2, 1918*

Address, 20 Bishop's Building, Salt Lake City, Utah

Heber J. Grant,   } *Editors*   Edward H. Anderson, *Business M*
Edward H. Anderson, }   Moroni Snow, *Assistant*

TABLE OF CONTENTS

"The Man of Tomorrow"

a wonderful new book on "Vocational Guidance"

By

Claude Richards

a successful business man,

will help every young man and woman in the selection of their life work. It is suited for young and old, and should be read by every parent.

"Vocational Guidance," as outlined in Claude Richards' book, is insurance against failure and a short cut to success.

This book should be in every home. It has been adopted for supplementary reading by the state schools and also by the Church schools.

The book is substantially bound in red vellum; it is printed on good paper, is profusely illustrated and has 296 pages. The price is extremely low—ONLY $1, postpaid $1.10.

Mail your order today to the

Improvement Era Office

20-23 Bishop's Building,   -   Salt Lake City, Utah

America's Most Distinguished Material For Memorials

"Used in such famous memorials as the Joseph Smith at Sharon, Vermont; the Hyrum Smith at Salt Lake City; the Philip D. Armour at Chicago; the "Uncle Joe" Cannon Family memorial at Danville, Ill.; the U. S. Senator Gordon at Los Angeles, Cal.; and thousands of others.

"See your dealer for further information, or write for free booklet, "The Rock of Ages."

Boutwell, Milne & Varnum Company,

Dept. O., Montpelier, Vermont.

"QUARRIES AT BARRE, VT.,
THE GRANITE CENTER OF THE WORLD"